MW00668875

Architecture A to Z

An Elemental, Alphabetical Guide to Kansas City's Built Environment

STEVE PAUL

A pedestrian path, incorporating an old railroad bridge, connects Union Station with the Freight House and the Crossroads Arts District.

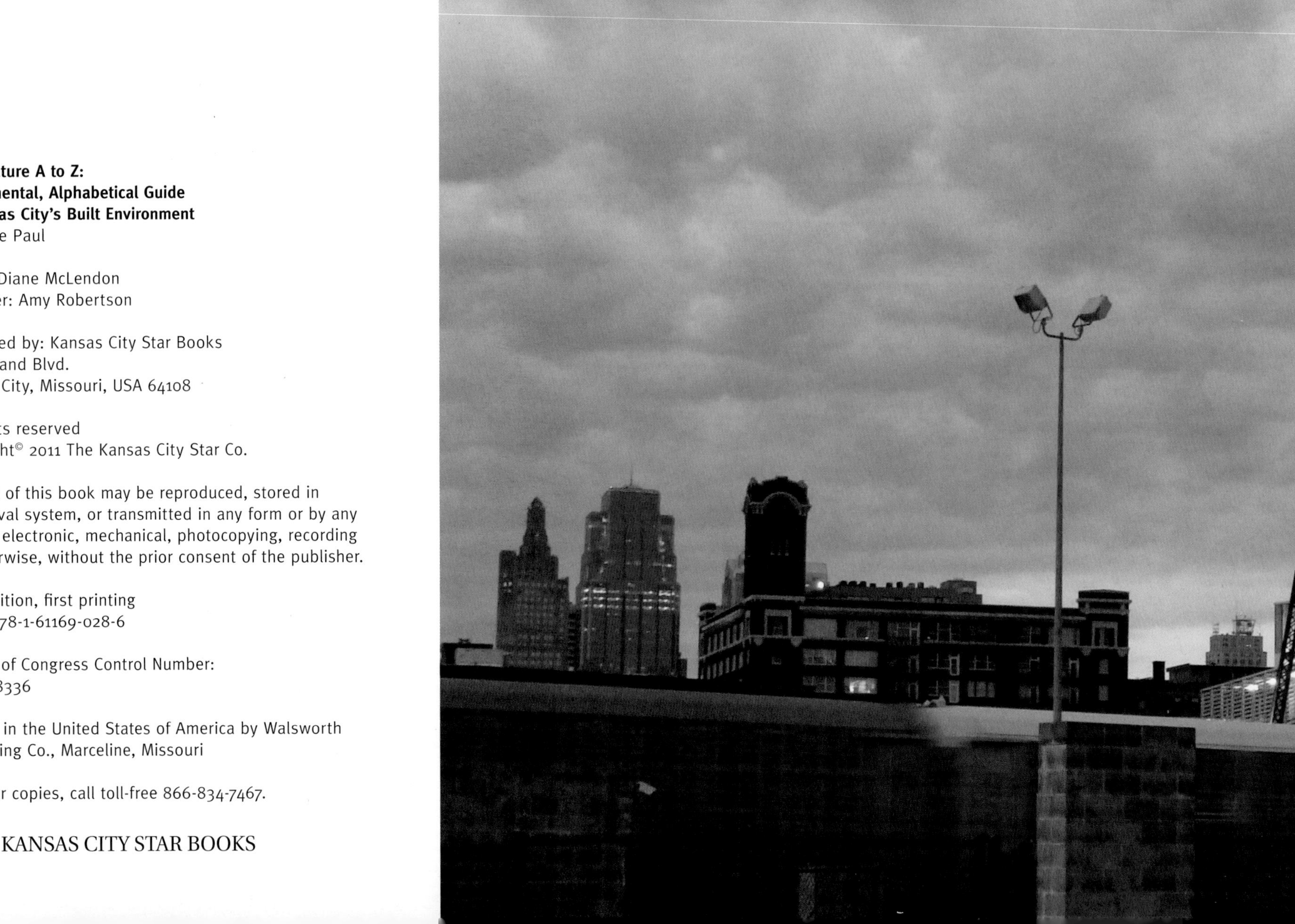

Architecture A to Z:
An Elemental, Alphabetical Guide
to Kansas City's Built Environment
By Steve Paul

Editor: Diane McLendon
Designer: Amy Robertson

Published by: Kansas City Star Books
1729 Grand Blvd.
Kansas City, Missouri, USA 64108

First edition, first printing
ISBN: 978-1-61169-028-6

Library of Congress Control Number:
2011938336

Printed in the United States of America by Walsworth Publishing Co., Marceline, Missouri

To order copies, call toll-free 866-834-7467.

KANSAS CITY STAR BOOKS

Contents

BELGER
Cartage Service Inc

Introduction

Kansas City has grown from a rough riverside settlement into a sprawling metropolis in the blink of two centuries.

How we move about the city now, how we enjoy it as a place and admire what makes it distinctive are individual things. They depend on who we—or you—are. Our experience of the city depends on our individual histories, on the paths we've gone down in our personal and cultural lives. It depends on whether we actually take the time to read the city as we live, work and play in it.

Nearly three years ago, I set out to discover some of the things that make Kansas City what it is. How did we get from there to here? If you pick through the visible bones of the city's past, what would you find? And, most important for the purpose of this exercise—a magazine series we called "Architecture A-Z"—what role does architecture play in creating the experience of Kansas City?

"We all see more of architecture than of any other art," the English journalist C.E. Montague once wrote. "Every street is a gallery of architects' work."

Yet I'd venture to say that architecture is far from the minds of most Kansas Citians. We don't dwell on the notion that the space we live in was shaped by architects. We take architecture and design for granted. We rarely consider that choices have been made—choices based on money, laws, taste, time, materials, status and whimsy.

Every now and then, most often amid an atmosphere of controversy, architecture becomes a thing worthy of public discussion.

A view of the downtown skyline from the Liberty Memorial deck.

This page: When it opened in 2007, the Nelson-Atkins Museum of Art's Bloch Building changed the landscape and visitors' experience with art and architecture. Opposite: Downtown, evening, a blend of old and new.

The recent spat over a proposed office building on the Country Club Plaza, for example, is all about architecture and its associated activities—urban design, city planning, public place making, commercial redevelopment. When is architecture good or bad? What of our past should be preserved or protected? How much power should developers wield? These are vital questions, prompted by the Plaza proposal, that ought to be asked more often.

The revival of Kansas City's downtown in the last two decades is the story of architecture as an expression of corporate desire, civic pride and political infighting.

One of my favorite memorable architectural moments of recent years was the dustup former Mayor Kay Barnes created as she was about to anoint Frank Gehry as the designer of a downtown arena. A consortium of local sports architects and experienced arena designers (Gehry, a hockey fan, had yet to design one) took offense at the intrusion and quickly put together a team that wrested the project from the clutches of the convention-exploding visionary.

As a result, of course, the locals helped to avoid the kind of eye-popping, crowd-attracting and budget-challenging marvel Gehry has notably planted elsewhere. Instead of the kind of physiological stir Gehry typically delivers, we got, in the Sprint Center, an inoffensive glass bowl that works reasonably well but sits a bit heavy on the streetscape. It's classic, conservative, soft-spoken Kansas City.

The idea of architecture as aesthetic invention and unique experience came to the fore a dozen years ago when trustees of the Nelson-Atkins Museum of Art chose designer Steven Holl's plan to expand the museum with a glass-topped, underground palace of light. It was radical. And invigorating.

The resulting public discussions, debates and ultimate general acceptance of the Nelson's Bloch Building speak to the ability of architecture to stir our passions viscerally. If cultural structures built by star architects are the cathedrals of our day, then the soaring asymmetry of Holl's Bloch Building provides some of the most awe-inspiring spatial experiences we have in this city. Architecture's role as inducer of heart-pumping exuberance returns on the local landscape in the fall of 2011 (about the time this book is published) with the opening of the Kauffman Center for the Performing Arts, the bulbous, hilltop complex designed by architect Moshe Safdie.

The fact that Safdie, an international practitioner known for grand, refined and geometrically formal institutional gestures, is also responsible for designing one of our

"The power that elevates the science of building into the domain of architecture and makes it a fine art is the same power that converts prose into poetry. This is a creative power, which refines expression with beauty of form, and illuminates reason with imagination."

—Henry Van Brunt, 1893

more disastrous recent building ventures is another one of those choice architectural moments, still unresolved, that's guaranteed to be talked about for years. I'm speaking, of course, about the West Edge office and hotel complex next to the Plaza, still standing naked and vacant like some concrete-skinned ruin as its fate awaits the actions of litigious bean counters and tireless deal makers.

All of this heavy cogitation on the meaning of architecture in our town came as a surprise to those who have regarded our long-running magazine project as a light-hearted diversion from the brain-cramping problems that assault us daily from all directions. But the "Architecture A-Z" project, which captured many snapshot views of Kansas City's past and present, also tried to touch on some of the major design issues of our time. It also proved to be a way of acknowledging that there is always,

Ornamental details can be filled with stylized foliage and mythological figures. Above: a terra cotta panel above the entry to 909 Walnut, formerly the Fidelity National Bank Building. Left: Capitals atop engaged, or embedded, columns at the former Covenant Baptist Church, Ninth and Harrison streets, feature acanthus leaves.

The tower base and sphinx at the Liberty Memorial.

and everywhere, more than meets the eye. That is one of its stronger messages, I hope: You can learn a lot if you slow down and look.

The idea for the project was relatively simple: March through the alphabet and look high and low for appropriate subjects and pictures to illuminate what makes this middle-coast place work. My aim was to make it fun, informative, interesting and, whenever possible, surprising.

The feature struck a chord. Many readers wrote and called to comment, to suggest ideas and to add to (or, alas, correct) the details. The word on the street was encouraging and gratifying. There seemed enough of a following to sustain a second run through the alphabet. And the discoveries kept emerging, sometimes at lightning speed as tight deadlines approached.

Asa Beebe Cross. Edgar Faris. John W. McKecknie. Joseph Radotinsky. Their names are rarely spoken today, but

An open-air columned park structure on Gladstone Boulevard is dedicated to George Kessler, who helped plan the city's parks and boulevards system.

each of these architects of the past helped give our metro area character and life. It was enlightening to trip across their names repeatedly and satisfying to highlight their contributions.

Selby Kurfiss? Who could've predicted that a distinctive arts and crafts house in Brookside came from an architect—Kurfiss—who is also credited with a rather plain brick commercial building that we now know and love as Arthur Bryant's?

Kansas City, like any other metropolis, can be a place of wonder.

Tom Nelson, the "N" in BNIM and one of the deans of Kansas City architecture today, remembers his first encounters with the city on boyhood drives from the family home in St. Joseph.

"I was a little kid during the war," he told me, "the war" being World War II. "The most exciting thing in my life at that time was coming to Kansas City, which you didn't do very often, because gas was rationed. You came down to meet someone at Union Station, an aunt or an uncle.

"I remember this very vivid image I had. You'd come down 71 Highway through Platte Woods or down 169 through Gladstone, which we did more of, and you came out at

Triangular motifs and glass ornaments made from common ashtrays dominate the living room in the Hyde House, designed by visionary Oklahoma architect Bruce Goff in the 1960s.

Oak Street. And you were looking right at downtown Kansas City, and particularly City Hall and the courthouse. And that image that stuck with me: this limestone—I didn't know the term 'art deco' then—this limestone city in that vernacular, whatever it was. I didn't know that word either—'vernacular.' But it was a very strong image.

"There was 911 Walnut and Kansas City Power & Light, and that's what the city was. I think it was kind of unusual. I don't think a lot of other cities had that kind of cohesion. A lot of that is left; those buildings are intact, and they're powerful enough that that feeling still exists."

Yes, we are the Limestone City. Kind of like the Emerald City, though paler. And like encountering that place from a teasing distance as the Yellow Brick Road unfurls, I think it's inspiring to spy the grand sweep of the city's skyline from miles away, as you can from high points in almost any direction. With some of the newer glass towers downtown, it even has a shade of emerald.

In addition to the long view of the central core, it's equally fun and eminently absorbing to look closely at the details, to consider the city stone by stone, as the 19th-century critic John Ruskin once suggested. So "Architecture A-Z" also presented an opportunity to celebrate distinctive ornaments, public sculptures, building parts and other microscopic features, without which we'd be just another generic, featureless nowhere. From Spanish-tinged filigree on the Plaza to corporate lions and eagles to boldly patterned, brick towers at Wyandotte High School—every detail tells a story.

Dan Maginn, another native of St. Joseph, represents the generation of architects following in Tom Nelson's footsteps. A principal in the firm of El Dorado Inc., Maginn is most excited by pieces of Kansas City that feel most

"Forget the damned motor car and build the cities for lovers and friends."

—Lewis Mumford, historian and architecture critic (1895-1990)

The Kauffman Center for the Performing Arts, north view, in morning sunlight.

authentic—original, organic expressions of urban living rather than Disneyfied recreations of a place long past.

Authenticity, Maginn says, requires a high quality human experience. “Something needs to be good—it can be food or music or a dramatic view—and number of things that make one happy to be alive or aware of being alive on the planet.”

Maginn’s firm is headquartered west of Broadway and Union Station and hard by the railroad tracks that are among the busiest in the nation. He and his partners have gotten used to the rumble. “That’s authentic,” he says, “and it hasn’t been branded.”

Maginn recalls the days in the late 1990s when an old warehouse behind Union Station was a scary shell of a place and Dan Clothier, a developer with roots in Wichita, began talking about transforming it into a restaurant.

“Everyone was telling him he was crazy,” Maginn says.

Not only did Clothier open one restaurant, the former City Tavern, but he attracted two more prominent and highly successful ones—Fiorella's Jack Stack Barbecue and Lidia's Kansas City—to become tenants in what's known as the Freight House.

"That's a testament to someone not trying to recreate something," Maginn says. "It's a vision of something not done before. A no-brainer. It's a unique experience, and few people saw that except for him."

The vibrancy of a city depends on how open it is to the work and influence of visionaries. The men who laid out our system of parks and boulevards certainly qualify. J.C. Nichols, who planned the Plaza and any number of long-lasting institutions nearby, is widely revered for what he contributed to the city's idea of itself (though the legacy of whites-only restrictive covenants in Nichols neighborhoods must also not be forgotten).

And let's not overlook the artists and place-makers who have been in the vanguard of the city's cultural ascendancy of the last 20 years.

The city's architectural future seems to be in good hands as well.

I've gotten close-up views recently as architecture students at the University of Kansas and Kansas State University have tackled projects meant to inject life into forgotten or underused sections of the central city.

The KU studio, under the guidance of Josh Shelton, one of Maginn's colleagues at El Dorado, spent a semester considering what to do with an Interstate 35 corridor near downtown—the land beneath the highway overpass that divides the Crossroads and West Side neighborhoods between 17th Street and Southwest Boulevard. Can it be reclaimed for housing or a water park and wetlands? All it would take to adopt one or more of those ambitious plans is civic vision and money.

The K-State students, led by Vladimir Krstic at the Kansas City Design Center, made a deep analysis of the West Bottoms and have proposed a series of fundamental and highly rational interventions—from riverfront soccer fields to a new transit hub—that would help bring that 19th-century industrial district into the 21st.

Another student venture, the Studio 804 project, an offshoot of KU's architecture department under the direction of Dan Rockhill, has brought cutting-edge and environmentally sensitive technologies to a series of outstanding modernist houses in Kansas City, Kan. Their efforts in KCK and in tornado-recovery projects in Greensburg, Kan., have attracted significant national attention.

And UMKC's Department of Architecture, Urban Planning and Design, now housed in an architecturally significant, 1960s-era building on campus, has grown into a reliable and creative source of deep thinking about city planning here and elsewhere.

In other words, Kansas City's architectural community, which has seen great accomplishment and wrenching economic challenges of late, is well prepared to shape the space we live in from here on out—all the way from A to Z, that is. For the rest of us, all we need to do as we read the city our builders make is to stop, listen and look.

—Steve Paul, July 2011

About the Photographs

When it launched in The Kansas City Star Magazine, "Architecture A-Z," clearly was intended to be a visual feature. It quickly turned into a photographic journey, and my deadline planning for each entry often was driven by the photographs I could take in my travels around town. Although a few pictures in this book come from The Star's files or from architects and others, most are my own. As an amateur photographer, I wasn't interested in, or equipped for, setting up architectural beauty shots. Nor did I want to offend the sensibilities of photographic professionals. Mostly I ended up shooting pictures with available light (and shadows). I am cognizant of the warning that architect Tom Nelson uttered in conversation one day that taking pictures often gets in the way of seeing. But I am hopeful that it's possible to do both. And hopeful, too, that, freed of the limited space of a one-page, multi-picture feature, some of the photographs stand on their own as worthy glimpses of the city's architectural life.

—SP

Opposite: Interior view of the Kauffman Center's Brandmeyer Great Hall.

D. THAYER CO.-WAR

A

ARENA

The concept of public gathering spaces for entertainment hasn't changed much in 2,000 years: tiered seats arranged around a stage for athletics or theater. The amphitheater at Pompeii sat 12,000 in an ovoid bowl. Kansas City's Sprint Center (above; 2007), a $250 million project, seats about 18,000. The Municipal Auditorium (1935) has also been upgraded in recent years. The fate of Kemper Arena (1974) in the West Bottoms remains uncertain.

ASB UNDERPASS

A long-standing obstacle in a hiking and biking trail along the Missouri River north of downtown gave way in January 2010 with the opening of this crucial connector below the ASB Railroad Bridge. BNIM and Taliaferro & Browne designed the project for the Port Authority. It includes concrete walkways, stone walls and river overlooks.

AIRPORT
When it opened in 1973, Kansas City International Airport, designed by the firm of Kivett and Myers, was among the first three-concourse projects. The scheme made for easy access for travelers. Will it stay that way? Our 21st-century emphasis on heightened security has prompted discussion about revising the airport plan.

ALLEYS
Downtown Kansas City is webbed by alleys, which are generally overlooked and underused as pedestrian-oriented public spaces. But what an opportunity. The spaces between many buildings, especially those that connect streets and continue for more than a block or two, have the potential to be far more useful than the typical void in which to park cars and trash receptacles. Flea markets? Street musicians? Inviting walkways or vest-pocket parks?

This reclaimed alley, connecting Baltimore Avenue and Wyandotte Street, just south of 10th Street, may be a test project in the making. Adjacent to the Kansas City Design Center, the narrow urban park is home to two public artworks as part of the Art in the Loop program. Ready. Set. Activate.

ART DECO

Art Deco is a style of the early 20th century characterized by sleek, decorative lines and visible in many high-profile buildings of the 1930s. Examples include the Kansas City Power & Light Building (interior detail above; 1931), Fidelity Bank (1932) and public structures such as the Jackson County Courthouse (1934), Municipal Auditorium (1935) and City Hall (1937).

ARMOUR BOULEVARD

This tree-lined midtown Kansas City roadway once boasted some of the most fashionable homes and apartment buildings in town. Kirkland B. Armour, of the meat-packing company, built a mansion at Armour and Warwick boulevards circa 1893. The Kansas City Star once referred to the French chateau-style home, razed in the 1930s, as “the most pretentious ever erected here.” Its site now belongs to the Foreign Language Middle School. Elegant apartment buildings sprouted along the boulevard in the early 20th century. Those include the Ellison (designed by architect Nelle E. Peters), near Broadway, and three glamour buildings, at Gillham Road, that are being renovated and reopened as apartments. The art deco detail (pictured) of one of those buildings, Clyde Manor, is a typically stylish gesture that can still be seen along Armour between Broadway and Troost Avenue.

ARCH

An arch is the span across the top of an opening, often curved, semicircular (Roman) or pointed (Gothic), and usually constructed to support a load or large wall expanse. A series of arches lining an open walkway is an arcade (see the Colosseum in Rome); arches applied decoratively to a wall compose a blind arcade. On the Country Club Plaza, arched windows alternate with blind arches along 47th Street in the building housing Pottery Barn and Barnes & Noble. A contemporary downtown office building pays respect to a Roman arch in its doorway and window design (far left). The Rosedale Arch (left), a World War I memorial built in Kansas City, Kan., in 1923, echoes the Arc de Triomphe, a Paris landmark built a century earlier.

ASAI ARCHITECTURE

The successor firm to Abend Singleton Associates and now merged with PGAV Architects, ASAI and principal Stephen Abend have been involved in the design of a slew of notable area projects. Major ones include the Charles Evans Whittaker U.S. Court House (1998) and the Liberty Memorial restoration (2006), which created a museum and other public spaces underground (right) and won a national honor award from the American Institute of Architects. Other projects in the Abend and ASAI portfolio include the United Missouri Bank Headquarters (1986) and Missouri Court of Appeals (1983).

BATTLEMENTS

Someone must've thought it was a good idea to fringe the upper regions of the twin American Century towers, at 45th and Main streets, with these throwbacks to medieval castles. Perhaps a subtle nod to security? Or a gesture of whimsical post-modernism?

To me, this prominent, though flimsy, decorative flourish (on buildings I've never much liked) seems as sincere as a clip-on tie. In contrast, the battlements feel more natural on the low-lying former bank building (now Architectural Salvage, inset) on Southwest Boulevard. For the record, a battlement, also known as crenellation, is a notched parapet alternating merlons (the uprights) and crenels, from where arrows and bullets were flung.

BNIM ARCHITECTS

One of the largest and most influential architectural firms in Kansas City, BNIM was founded in 1970 and has built a reputation for its commitment to environmentally conscious and responsible architecture and design. Its highest-profile projects of recent years include the Lewis and Clark State Office Building (2005) in Jefferson City, the School of Nursing at the University of Texas in Houston (with Lake Flato, 2004), the IRS Kansas City Regional Center (with 360 Architecture, 2006), the Nelson-Atkins Museum of Art expansion and renovation (with Steven Holl, 2007) and the Kauffman Performing Arts Center (with Moshe Safdie, 2011). The firm's initials stand for founding or longtime principals: Bob Berkebile, Tom Nelson, David Immenschuh and Steve McDowell. In 2011 the American Institute of Architects recognized BNIM as firm of the year.

BMA TOWER

The Chicago firm of Skidmore, Owings and Merrill designed this local landmark for the Business Men's Assurance Co. in the early 1960s. Its distinctive feature, aside from the highly visible hilltop site overlooking Penn Valley Park, is the external structure, or exoskeleton, which frames the dark, glass-walled core. A legal battle ensued in the mid-1980s after some of the original marble panels fell off the building and the skin was replaced by synthetic glass (or neoparium) tiles. Of late, the building has been in the process of transformation from office space to luxury condos (now known as One Park Place).

BOLEY BUILDING
This six-story historic treasure at 1130 Walnut St. opened in 1909. Designed by architect Louis S. Curtiss, it's an early example of curtain-wall construction – the glass façade is supported by cantilevered floor plates rather than being part of an external structural frame. The building recently underwent a $19 million renovation and is now occupied by publisher Andrews McMeel Universal.

BOARD OF TRADE
The city's first Board of Trade building (1877) still stands as a condo complex at 502 Delaware St. The second, at 210 W. Eighth St. (pictured), was demolished in 1968, a devastating blow in Kansas City preservation history. The 1888 structure bore the elaborate ornament and stunning entry arch associated with the Chicago firm of Burnham and Root. A third building, at 10th and Wyandotte, now houses condos. In 1966 the grain exchange moved to its current building at 4800 Main St.

BUNKER BUILDING

Described as Victorian eclectic and saved from demolition in the 1970s, this limestone and brick commercial building (architect unknown) went up at 820 Baltimore Ave. in 1881. It originally housed a printing concern owned by Walter A. Bunker. In its block, terminating on the south at Ninth Street below, the building contributes to a harmonious grouping that offers a glimpse into our urban past.

BRUSH CREEK TOWERS

When it opened in 1972, the apartment complex at 1800 Brush Creek Blvd. was the first Kansas City public housing project for elderly people. Designed by architect John Lawrence Daw and Associates, the federally funded structure boasted Euro-style design touches, including a skylighted atrium and a jaunty array of windows and exterior concrete panels.

BURNHAM AND ROOT

The Chicago architectural firm, led by Daniel Burnham and John Wellborn Root, left a legacy of sturdy and beautiful buildings across the Midwest. Seven of its projects rose in Kansas City in a boom period of the 1880s. Only one still stands, the onetime Scarritt residence at 3240 Norledge Ave. in the Northeast area of Kansas City (see page 80).

BRIDGES

Ten state highway bridges and three railroad bridges cross the Missouri River in the Kansas City area. Kansas City owes much of its prosperous history to a decision made by railroad interests in the 1860s to bridge the river here rather than upstream in St. Joseph. The stone-and-iron Hannibal Bridge (above left), partly designed by engineer Octave Chanute, opened in 1869 and, according to one account, led to the southward expansion of the city and the decline of commercial activity on the waterfront. The bridge was replaced in 1917; that structure still stands just east of the Broadway Bridge (above right).

B

MARCEL BREUER

In 1953, Robert Snower and his wife saw a magazine article about a Connecticut house designed by this major 20th-century architect, designer and teacher. They wanted him to build them one, too. Breuer, a onetime associate of the Bauhaus, never saw the Snowers' Mission Hills lot on Belinder Road, but he delivered to them this now-classic, modernist design. Completed in 1955, it seems to float above the site. The house features redwood siding and Breuer-designed furnishings, such as this chair and built-in cabinetry.

COTE

The American Institute of Architects' Committee on the Environment each year names a list of the most exemplary projects adhering to principles of sustainability and eco-conscious design. BNIM of Kansas City received one of 10 awards for 2010, for the campus building and wastewater treatment facility at the Omega Center for Sustainable Living (2009), in Rhinebeck, N.Y.

LOUIS CURTISS

This Canadian transplant (1865-1924) became one of Kansas City's most distinguished architects. In addition to his famous Boley Clothing Co. Building, his legacy here reflects the major design styles of the early 20th century and includes the Clay County Bank (1906) in Excelsior Springs, the Bernard Corrigan residence (1912-13) at 55th Street and Ward Parkway (northwest corner), the art nouveau-influenced Mineral Hall (1903-05) at the KC Art Institute and his own studio building (pictured) at 1118-20 McGee Street (1908-09), where he lived upstairs.

CONCRETE

New technologies in concrete construction have led to all sorts of cost-efficient, energy-saving and creative, new applications of the age-old material.

Moldable into a variety of forms when wet, hard and monolithic when dry, concrete comprises aggregates of broken stone and sand, water and cement. The ancient Romans built with it; so did the makers of the Great Wall of China. And what would Kansas City be without the civic construction spree of the Tom Pendergast era? After all, he did own the Ready-Mixed Concrete Co.

Today concrete is one of the most-used building materials. Gaining strength from admixtures, steel reinforcement and pre-stressing, it can be used for the most basic to the most dynamic of building types.

Cast-in-place concrete is the process of making structural beams, columns, floors and walls by pouring the wet material into formworks in the final location. You can see this type on the surface of roads, bridges, building structures and retaining walls. (Note the entry pavilion at the Sulgrave Regency complex, 1965, pictured here.)

Precast concrete is produced in off-site manufacturing plants; products include wall-cladding panels (see the IRS Regional Service Center, 2006, pictured), ornamental detailing, roof tiles and concrete blocks.

Concrete retaining walls at the Nelson-Atkins Museum's Bloch Building are patterned with imprints of rip-sawn boards.

COMMUNITY CHRISTIAN CHURCH

Another concrete tale: When Frank Lloyd Wright's plan to use a sprayed concrete called Gunite over an unusual steel and paper frame ran into trouble with city building officials, he divorced himself from the project. Architect Edward Buehler Delk took over, made revisions, and the church (pictured opposite) was completed in 1941.

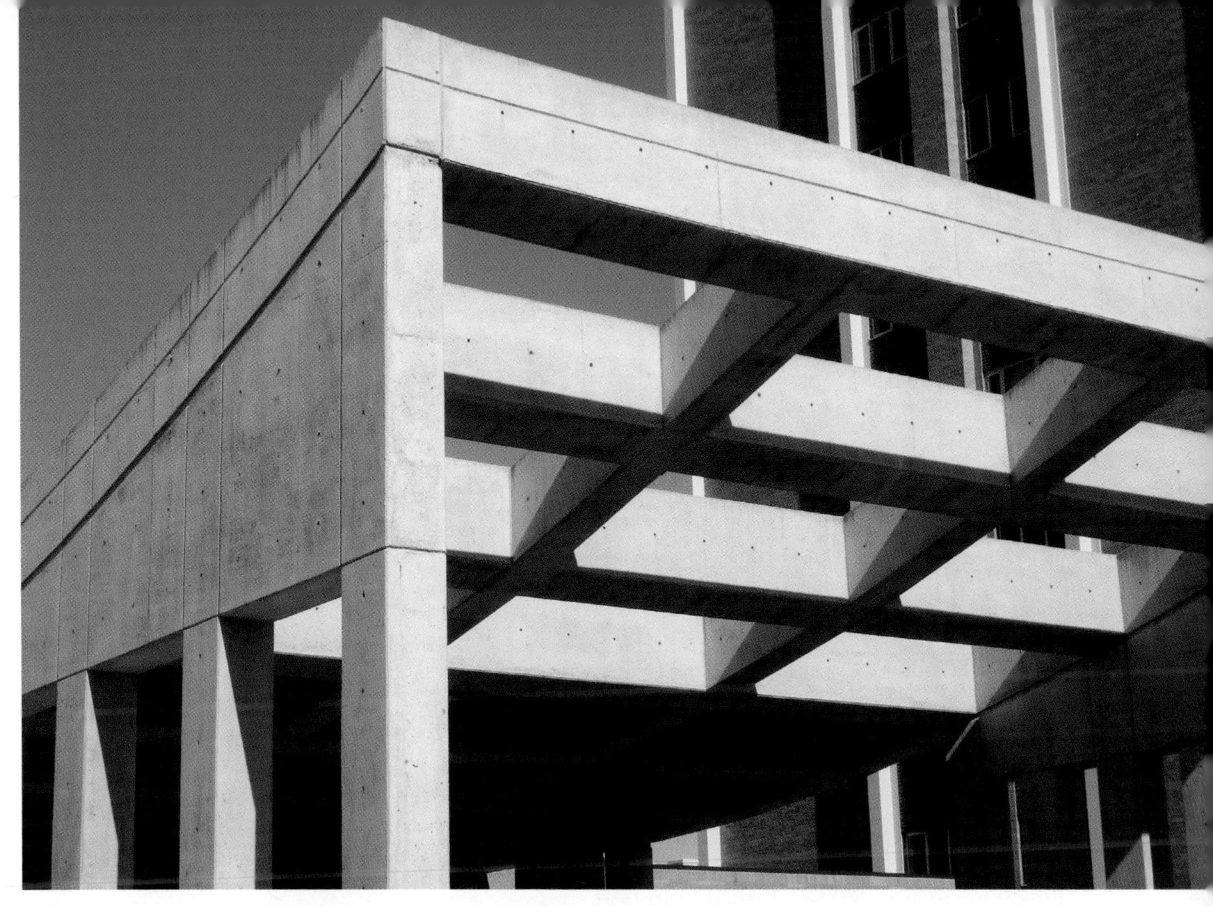

ASA BEEBE CROSS

When he arrived in Kansas City about 1858, this New Jersey native (1826-1894) launched a lumberyard at Eighth and Main streets. He also designed buildings, and by the 1870s had become the most prominent architect in town. His name was attached to some of the city's most important 19th-century buildings, including the original Union Depot (1878) in the West Bottoms and the first Jackson County Courthouse (1872; destroyed by tornado in 1886). The most notable buildings by Cross still standing include the exuberantly Victorian Vaile Mansion (1881) in Independence, the Pacific House Hotel (1868) in the River Market (see pages 25 and 76-77) and St. Patrick's Catholic Church (1874-75), Eighth and Cherry streets (left).

COVENANT BAPTIST CHURCH

The Chicago architects Willoughby Edbrooke and Franklin Pierce Burnham (apparently no relation to architect Daniel Burnham) are identified with the Richardsonian Romanesque style, as can be seen in the rounded arches, stonework and other details of this distinctive yet mostly ignored building at Ninth and Harrison streets. Members of the original Calvary Baptist Church laid the cornerstone in 1888. A fire in 1948 destroyed the interior and a distinctively gabled roof; the insides were rebuilt.

CORINTHIAN HALL 

Mansion is hardly the word for this plush showplace, which after completion in late 1910 became the 70-room home of lumber baron R.A. Long and his family. The Gladstone Boulevard outpost of the Kansas City Museum is undergoing extensive, stripped-to-the-bones restoration, a project expected to last five years or more. Henry Hoit was the architect, touching all the luxurious Euro bases of the Beaux-Arts, neo-classical style of the day.

Corinthian Hall got its name from the six 25-foot columns that hold up the portico, each topped by the elaborately detailed capitals of the most effusive of the three Greek "orders" of classical architecture.

COMMUNITY OF CHRIST AUDITORIUM AND TEMPLE

Call this Independence complex, at River and Walnut streets, the Dome, the Spire and the Pipes. The auditorium dates to 1926; the temple designed by what's now HOK Inc., opened in 1994. Between them, the structures contain organs comprising about 12,000 pipes.

D

EDWARD BUEHLER DELK

Developer J.C. Nichols brought this consulting architect to town to devise the original plan for the Country Club Plaza in 1922. Delk's tour of Seville, Spain, along with travels to Mexico, cemented his vision of stucco buildings, tile motifs and similar details, which characterize the Plaza look. Delk (1885-1956) designed the Tower Building and other Plaza structures. But his legacy in Kansas City also includes significant houses on both sides of the state line; D.W. Newcomer's Sons (1925), 1331 Brush Creek Pkwy.; the charming Linwood-Paseo traffic island (c. 1931); St. Andrews Episcopal Church (1931, right); and Starlight Theatre (1951). He worked with Frank Lloyd Wright on Community Christian Church (1940) and the Sondern house (1940, 1950) near Roanoke Park.

DRAWING

In an online slideshow for Slate magazine, the writer and architecture critic Witold Rybczynski once rhapsodized about the drawings of Louis Kahn. He suggested that the esteemed architect's stripped-down modernism and seemingly quaint sketching style could be seen as antidotes to our recent period of irrational building excess. Architects and engineers today have incredibly efficient tools—computer modeling in two and three dimensions, for example—allowing the construction of ever more difficult and expressive buildings. But even those projects tend to start on paper, as many practitioners still hold onto old-fashioned drawing by hand. Above: Moshe Safdie's early sketch of the Kauffman Center for the Performing Arts.

DELAWARE STREET

The River Market area contains some of downtown's oldest buildings and the largest concentration of relatively intact 19th-century commercial streetscapes. Take a four-block walk on this street, from Second Street southward, and sense the vestiges of historic Kansas City (even as modern buildings and redos nestle in). The historic Pacific House (1868), once a hotel, stands at 401 Delaware St. Across the street, the narrow, stone-clad building at 310 Delaware is all that remains of a larger structure erected circa 1867.

DENTIL

A dentil is a closely spaced, tooth-like motif, usually placed beneath a cornice, as in the trim above the lower windows of this 1920s-era Gillham Road apartment building and high and low at 310 Delaware (right).

JAMES P. DAVIS HALL

Back in that other deep recession/depression, the federal Works Progress Administration launched building and employment projects to keep hard-hit Americans working. Among the lasting results on the Kansas side of the metro area are numerous stone structures in the parklands surrounding Wyandotte County Lake, including shelters, culverts and bridges. (The 400-acre lake was also a WPA-funded project, its construction interrupted and drawn out for years after the nearly completed original dam collapsed in 1937.) Davis Hall (1937) was built from rough-hewn stone and wood gathered on the site. The rustic recreation hall, with its oak and black walnut interior, remains a popular site for weddings and other events.

DRUMMOND HOUSES

Builder Donald Drummond put up numerous houses in Johnson County and Kansas City neighborhoods in the 1950s and '60s, most of them ranch-style designs created for modern suburban tastes. This Prairie Village residence was designed by California architects A. Quincy Jones and Frederick Emmons, and it's one of perhaps seven of their Castilian plans built in the area. Like many other so-called Drummond houses, its airy, light-filled interior opens up to patios and the outdoors in elegant, refreshing ways. Just right for California dreaming in the heartland.

DUNN HEADQUARTERS

The J.E. Dunn Construction Co. outgrew its previous home and, aided by city-backed bonds and tax-increment-financing, built this six-story headquarters building on the east flank of Ilus Davis Park. The Dunn building opened in September 2009. The architect was a consortium of BNIM and 360 Architecture, a team similar to that responsible for the new IRS Regional Center. The gently curving glass wall overlooks the park and provides Dunn employees wide vistas of downtown. (That's the Whittaker U.S. Courthouse at the north end of the civic mall.) On the inside, design features include a salvaged-barnwood lobby floor, wonkily deployed high-efficiency fluorescent lights, lots of daylighting, an open office environment, and two-block-long hallways that avoid the effects of monstrous scale by bending softly in a calming arc.

E

EAGLES

There was much confusion early in the 20th century about which artist was responsible for the bronze eagle sculpture placed above the entrance to the New York Life Insurance Co. building at 20 W. Ninth St.—Augustus Saint-Gaudens or his brother, Louis. Later evidence points to the lesser-known Louis, but regardless, the eagle remains one of Kansas City's favorite historic pieces of public art. A symbol of strength, of course, the eagle was commonly employed for commercial as well as federal branding. A block away, eagle ornaments appear at 21 W. 10th St. and next door at 15 W. 10th.

EIGHTEEN EIGHTY-EIGHT

Kansas City's population in 1880 was about 63,000. By the end of the decade it had more than doubled, and with that influx of people came prosperity and a building boom. The boom peaked about 1888, which was the birth year of bunches of buildings, a few still standing, though in varying degrees of health: the Blossom House, 1032 Pennsylvania Ave.; St. Mary's Episcopal Church, 1307 Holmes St.; the Chicago, Milwaukee and St. Paul Railroad Depot, known today as the Freight House; and the down-on-its-luck Covenant Baptist Church, 821 Harrison St. The New York Life Building, where this 1888 plaque is located, was completed in 1890. One more thing: In the 1880s, the number of architects in Kansas City almost tripled, from 22 to 65.

ENTABLATURE

In classical architecture, entablature comprises a horizontal grouping of details sitting atop columns, as in this local example in the 1100 block of Grand Boulevard. Each element of the entablature has a technical name, of course, including the larger pieces (from bottom to top of the group) architrave, frieze, dentil band (the teethlike molding) and cornice.

EGYPTIAN REVIVAL

Architect John W. McKecknie was a prominent Kansas City designer in the early decades of the 20th century (see page 66), producing a long record of midtown apartments, downtown offices and other structures in eclectic styles of the day. For the Stine and McClure Undertaking Co. in 1912, he produced this two-story building at 924 Oak St. (now Siegrist Engraving Co.), its details and adornments reflecting motifs from ancient Egypt. You can find the Egyptian Revival influence in art deco settings around the area and at the Liberty Memorial, pictured here with one of a pair of hooded sphinxes guarding the monument and museum halls.

ELLERBE BECKET
This firm traces its roots to a Minneapolis practice that opened more than 100 years ago. In 1988, Ellerbe and Associates merged with a California firm, Welton Becket Associates, and opened a Kansas City office. In 2009 the firm became part of the global engineering and architecture company AECOM. The firm's local influence can be seen in projects ranging from Hallmark Cards' corporate headquarters (1950-55) to the Sprint Center and the Federal Reserve Bank of Kansas City (2008). Its offices, at 2380 McGee St., are part of a complex designed by the Chicago office of Ludwig Mies van der Rohe.

EYE FOUNDATION OF KANSAS CITY
Leawood architect Teh Kon Hu (later of Hu Jarvis Meyer) designed this postmodern assemblage of geometric forms and classical references in 1987. Architectural historian George Ehrlich cited the building, on Hospital Hill, as an "adventurous" counterpoint to Kansas City's traditionally conservative architectural leanings.

ELEVATION
Elevation is a rendering that shows the vertical features of a building, such as this section of the West-facing elevation of the Nelson Atkins' Bloch Building.

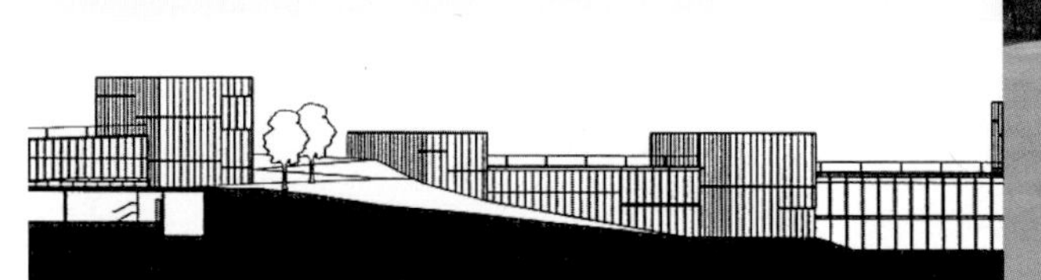

ELECTRIC PARK
On a spring day in 1907, the beer-making Heim brothers opened a wildly popular amusement park at the city's edge, at 46th Street and the Paseo. With a swimming beach and 100,000 light bulbs, the park was also home to an ornate band shell. According to lore, no less an expert than bandleader John Philip Sousa himself pronounced it the finest anywhere. Therein, no doubt, he set the precedent for world-class expectations in local concert halls. Electric Park closed after the 1925 season.

EPA BUILDINGS
When the Environmental Protection Agency's Science and Technology Center (right) opened in 2003 on Third Street in Kansas City, Kan., it became the first significant area building to earn LEED certification for its energy-efficient and environmentally conscious features. Two blocks and a few overpasses away, in 1999 the EPA placed its Region VII headquarters in a commercially developed building at Fifth Street and Minnesota Avenue (above). In 2011, the EPA announced it would move its headquarters to Lenexa, setting off heated debate and a legal challenge.

F

FENESTRATION

Fenestration is the design and placement of windows and other openings. Pictured: A sunset-painted AMC headquarters tower, built as Ten Main Center in 1968. Designed by Los Angeles architect Charles Luckman, the building has beveled windows that, according to historian George Ehrlich, marked a sculptured transition from the flat-surfaced styles of typical 1960s office buildings.

FIDELITY BANK BUILDING

As its draftsmen worked on the landmark Kansas City Power & Light Building, the firm of Hoit, Price & Barnes also got the job of designing a new headquarters for Fidelity National, now known as 909 Walnut, a condo tower. The twin-eared structure (1931), rising 465 feet from the sidewalk, was clad in granite and Indiana limestone and included much terra-cotta ornamentation, such as this scenic panel.

FEDERAL RESERVE BANK

This regional headquarters building opened in 2008 off Main Street just south of Liberty Memorial. Designed by the international firm of Pei Cobb Freed and Partners, along with Ellerbe Becket, the limestone and glass tower also houses the kid-friendly Money Museum.

EDGAR C. FARIS

Later in life, Edgar C. Faris (1881-1945) became known as an accomplished painter, and you might still find his landscapes hanging in old Country Club Plaza area apartment buildings. A portrait he made of Harry S. Truman was hanging in the White House the year Faris died.

But before that, Faris spent some time as an architect, back when that was an unlicensed activity in Missouri. He did some work for the city of Kansas City and left at least two notable private structures on our local streetscape. This Mediterranean-inspired villa (1924) stands on 52nd Street east of Loose Park. The Ponce de Leon apartment building (1925, now condos) still stands at 46th and Main streets. Its "rooftop bungalow" penthouse was once described as "the most ornate in the city." Faris is also responsible for another Spanish-style apartment building in midtown, the Alcazar (1925), and you can still see vestiges of the Moorish-Near Eastern details of a rug import business he designed in the façade and rooftop of the Gojo Japanese Restaurant (1923) on Broadway.

FOUNTAINS

In the 1940s, fountains and mirror pools were built at Unity Village as part of the campus cooling system, and over the years additions turned it into one of the largest in this fountain-happy metro. It had been dry since sections of concrete collapsed in 2003, but a restoration project (see the rendering) brought water back to the fountain in September 2010.

At the other end of the local fountain spectrum stands a curiosity. While stopped recently at the aforementioned Ponce de Leon condos, I couldn't help capturing a portrait of a contemporary addition, its slyly named Fountain of Ewes (by sculptor Jim Myers). It might be kitsch, but it's our kitsch, and thousands of Main Street travelers pass by it daily and often smile.

"FORM FOLLOWS FUNCTION"
One of the great mottos of modern architecture was committed to print circa 1896 by Chicago's influential practitioner Louis Sullivan. Modernist architects extended the idea to fuel their disdain for any kind of ornament. These days the idea is difficult to discern as an operating principle, even though it still sounds pretty good.

"Sullivan's famous dictum has been cast aside in recent years as 'starchitects' have been more likely to follow their own rule: 'form follows me,'" says veteran architect David Greusel. "In other words, I'll decide what shape I want this building to be, then I'll figure out a way to stuff the things my client needs into it and call it good."

Greusel doesn't buy that point of view. But, he adds, "'form follows function' has been used in the past to justify the worst kind of pragmatic utilitarianism, which is as bad as or worse than self-indulgent form-making. Sullivan, who was a brilliant architect and a gifted artist, would have been horrified to see what banal, warehouse-like buildings have been brought forth in the name of 'form follows function.'"

FAÇADE
When the downtown skyscraper then known as the AT&T Town Pavilion went up in the late 1980s, it came with a parking garage that covered much of an adjacent block. Historic structures gave way, but as a gesture to downtown heritage, the garage builders incorporated the west-facing exterior wall, or façade, of the Jenkins Music Co. building in the 1200 block of Walnut Street.

f

FENCE

Usually, we put up structures of wood, iron or barbed wire to define the edges of property. The word, of course, comes down to us in history from "defense." But in a large, topiary-filled garden on Sunset Hill, south of the Plaza, this tree fence along a driveway stands as a playful – and fruitful – alternative. The combination of apple and pear trees includes some bamboo structure and requires extensive pruning, the owner says. And, indeed, in the fall, we are told, neighborhood children benefit from its harvest. Try doing that with barbed wire.

FLOURNOY HOUSE

One of the oldest structures in the metro area, this four-room brick house in Independence dates to 1826, when it was built by the Jones H. Flournoy family. Later owners added on, but the original structure was moved and reconstructed at least twice, most recently in 1989. It now stands as part of the Restoration Heritage Plaza, 1034 W. Lexington St., and given its association with early and controversial Independence history, it's also a stop on the Mormon Walking Trail.

G

GUADALUPE CENTER

This landmark community center and social service agency in the West Side neighborhood was built in 1936 in the Mission/Spanish Colonial Revival style. Its architects reportedly worked for the Fred Harvey Co., famous builder of railroad concessions and other structures throughout the Southwest.

GARMENT DISTRICT

This historic district on the west side of downtown once housed shirtmakers, dressmakers and the like. Many of the old warehouse buildings date to the late 1880s, including the Thayer Building, at 820 Broadway, designed by Walter C. Root (1884).

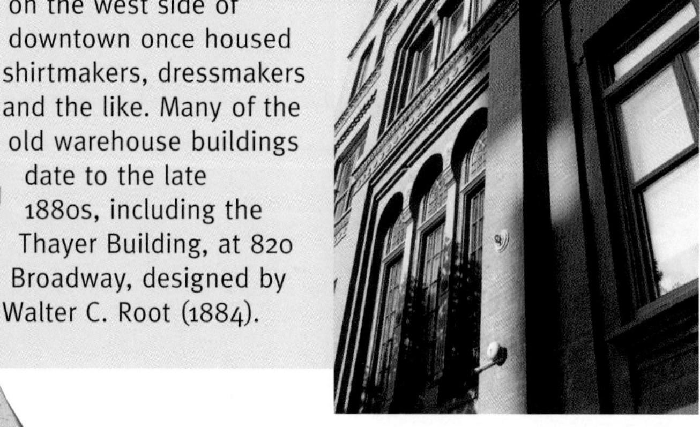

GARAGE

Perhaps more proper to call this a carriage house, but a garage is a garage, except when designed by Louis Curtiss. This one (1912-13), attached to a guest house behind Curtiss' famed Corrigan House at 55th Street and Ward Parkway, includes a swoopy art nouveau treatment.

GOLD

During a renovation in 1960 of the Cathedral of the Immaculate Conception, the original copper dome and spire got a new coat of 23-karat gold. On a cloudy gray day it can glow against the downtown sky. The site, on 10th Street off Broadway, has been home to a Catholic church since 1834, when Father Benedict Roux bought the land for $6.

GREENE & GREENE

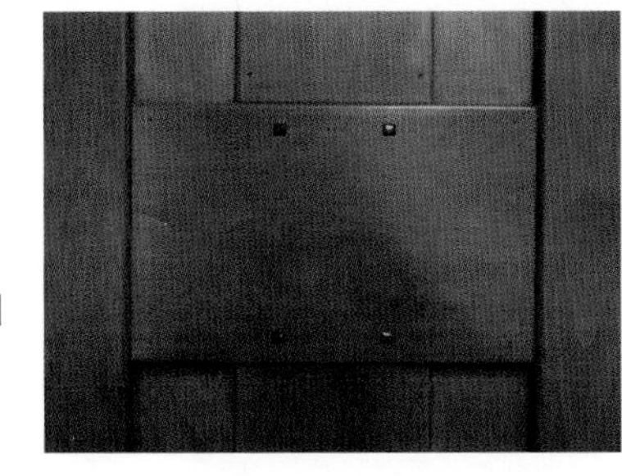

When the owners of 1000 Broadway wanted to renovate its entry hall in 2002, they envisioned a nod to Greene & Greene, the famed Pasadena, Calif., creators of Arts and Crafts-style homes and furnishings. Local craftsman Mark Parsons replicated the entry hall of the firm's Robert Blacker Estate, down to the finger joints, ebony plugs and the "cloud lifts" of the horizontal lines. The local version was made with stained alder and birch veneer; the original used mahogany. Principals of the California firm were two brothers, Charles and Henry Greene, who grew up and began their training in St. Louis. Pictured: Detail of the west entry wall paneling.

GUMBEL BUILDING

This six-story commercial structure at 801 Walnut St. dates to 1904. It's an early example of reinforced concrete construction, a specialty of its notable designer, John McKecknie. The building's west face is skinned with terra cotta, and other features include rounded, intricately adorned piers. Plans to convert the vacant building into condos have languished for several years.

FREDERICK C. GUNN

In the 1890s, this son of an engineer and bridge builder partnered with Louis Curtiss in an architectural practice that produced the Standard Theater (1900, now Folly) and, it's believed, the Sacred Heart Church (1896-97) at 2544 Madison Ave. (right). Curtiss went off on his own and became far better known. Yet Gunn practiced for another half century—he retired at age 85 and died, in 1959, at 93.

His career included some years designing "pompous Roman-arched courthouses, city halls and railroad stations," as The Kansas City Star once put it. He worked (as construction superintendent) on the Jackson County Courthouse (1934) and designed parts of the City Market and several buildings on Hospital Hill, including the old General Hospitals (1908, 1930).

As The Star also noted, he liked incorporating "reminders of the spirit behind the Greeks, the Romans, Shakespeare and the Victorian age." And, indeed, the ornamental inspiration above the entrance to General Hospital No. 1 quoted from Shakespeare's "Merchant of Venice": "The quality of mercy is not strained," it begins. That large building piece is all that remains of the old hospital; it stands as a historical marker in the 2300 block of Holmes Road.

BRUCE GOFF

This Kansas native (1904-1982) was largely a self-taught architect who is now considered a visionary modernist. He taught and practiced mostly in Oklahoma but spent six years in Kansas City in the 1960s. Here he designed three distinctly quirky homes: the small, open-plan Searing residence (1966, 1,200 square feet), lined on five of its six sides with glass (above and top right); the Hyde residence (1965), including accents made with store-bought, green-glass ashtrays (right, opposite top left, bottom left); and the Nicol house (1965-67), near the University of Missouri-Kansas City, an octagonal wonder with triangular windows and a sunken living-room conversation area surrounding a fountain/fire pit (opposite, top right).

G

HALLMARK

Los Angeles architect Welton Becket (part of the future firm of Ellerbe Becket) designed the card company's modern headquarters in 1950, and it opened five years later. Its boxy array of glass and relatively bland surfaces held up well over the years, historian George Ehrlich once wrote, as the company developed the adjacent Crown Center complex of high-rise hotels and office buildings.

H

HOWE RESIDENCE

Architect Frank M. Howe was a partner in the prominent Boston firm of Van Brunt & Howe, which established a Kansas City office in 1885. Two years later, he built this impressive Shingle-style home at 1707 Jefferson St. to showcase his firm's skills in residential buildings.

HARECLIFF

In 1921, the esteemed landscape architect Sid J. Hare built a rustic home—he called it Timbertent—on 21 acres in a natural setting on the southeast edge of town. He built a second small house a few steps away (lower right), which served as his office and later home to his daughter.

The houses of Harecliff adhered to principles of recycling that remain forward-thinking to this day. Big, heavy beams came from demolished wooden railroad bridges in Colorado. Sections of rough Carthage marble around his fireplace once did duty in post-wood, pre-concrete city sidewalks. The foundation and the chimney's organic tower of field stones (pictured then and now) came from the site itself. Hare surrounded the houses with flowers and birdsong, calling it a "safety zone for native plants and animals."

Harecliff enriched the historic setting near Cave Spring, a onetime campsite along the Santa Fe Trail.

"He was a proponent of preserving this area," said Sylvia Mooney, former leader of the Cave Spring Park Association and longtime resident of the Hare house at 7119 Harecliff Dr. "But he died in 1938, so he didn't live long enough to see it happen."

Through their celebrated firm of Hare & Hare, Sid Hare and his son Herbert shaped the landscape of important swaths of Kansas City (and elsewhere), including City Hall, the Nelson-Atkins Museum of Art and the Country Club Plaza district.

HARRIS-KEARNEY HOUSE

One of the oldest surviving structures in town, this Westport landmark was built by John and Henrietta Harris in 1855. It reflects the frontier simplicity and ambition of the day along with a nod to Greek Revival and other classical details. The house originally stood about a block away but was moved in 1922 to its current location, 4000 Baltimore Ave. Now it's home to a museum and the Westport Historical Society, which acquired the house in 1976.

HELPING HAND INSTITUTE

Built as institutional housing in 1915, this concrete and brick structure at 535 Grand Blvd., on the National Register of Historic Places, includes notable design features such as contrasting stone ornaments and carved wooden brackets at the cornice.

HNTB

Dating to 1914, this is one of the city's largest architecture, engineering and planning firms, and one of the country's top builders of bridges, roadways, airports and other huge civic projects. Formerly known as Howard Needles Tammen & Bergendoff, it accelerated its role as a local powerhouse in the 1970s by acquiring the influential firm of Kivett & Myers. Its local portfolio includes Bartle Hall (1976, 1994, 2007), KCI Airport and the Truman Sports Complex (1972-73), and its national projects stretch from the Maine Turnpike (since 1945) to the Tacoma, Wash., Narrows Bridge (2007). The firm has also put its stamp on venerable sports palaces and other projects around the globe.

H

HORTON'S OYSTER AND CHOP HOUSE
This River Market area landmark (507 Walnut St.), with an eye-catching array of façade details, dates to 1879.

MARY ROCKWELL HOOK
A product of the country club set, Hook (1877-1978) established her reputation as one of the city's few successful female architects by designing and building distinctive houses for family and friends. Influenced by extensive travels and studies in Chicago, Paris and elsewhere, Hook often used native stone excavated from the site, or a nearby Brush Creek quarry, and loved the asymmetry that building on a slope created. Find several examples in the Sunset Hill district, south of the Country Club Plaza, which she designed and built in the 1920s. Above: Hook designed her first house for herself, in 1908, though the siding, gingerbread and other details here came from later owners. Next came the big Bertrand Rockwell house (1908-09), built for her parents, on West 52nd Street, and later her longtime home at 4940 Summit Street (1925-27, detail).

I

ICON
A strict definition of "icon" limits its meaning to a representative image, especially a sacred one. But our loose language triumphs, and in the world of architecture, we more often think of icons as grand structures that stand out admirably or unabashedly from the conventional crowd and have the potential for defining the character of a place.

The Gateway Arch looms over St. Louis, of course, as one of the holiest of holy urban icons. But what about here? What makes an icon?

In Kansas City, we have such representative images as the Nelson-Atkins Shuttlecocks (1994), which in recent years have risen on the local status landscape, and the Hereford in the sky, which has declined a bit since moving to a less visible perch on the west edge of downtown.

It's sad that in the making of downtown Kansas City's skyline in the last eight or nine decades, not a single building competes on today's icon meter. As for great contemporary architectural statements, does Steven Holl's Bloch Building qualify? Nighttime beauty shots make it a candidate for iconicity.

Will Moshe Safdie's Kauffman Center for the Performing Arts become the hilltop, iconic symbol of our urban identity when it opens in the fall of 2011? Too soon to tell.

In the end, an icon involves a personal relationship—does it connect with you on an emotional or a sensory level? That relationship can be made more meaningful by community agreement. All it requires is looking and feeling connected.

INDUSTRIAL REVOLUTION STYLE
Spanning the latter half of the 18th century and most of the 19th, industrial buildings evolved as iron and steel became dominant framing materials, even for structures clad in masonry. The West Bottoms is dotted with 19th-century remnants of the period, such as this one.

INFILL
In urban development, the term refers to building on vacant land as a way to reconnect neighborhoods and enhance civic and pedestrian vitality. The Power & Light District, for example, is a huge infill project, encompassing more than six city blocks, most of which were dormant or blighted for years.

INDEPENDENCE AVENUE

If you want to understand local immigrant history, look no farther than here.

Running eastward from downtown Kansas City, Independence Avenue has served as a vital artery for newcomers for 100 years or more. Its melting-pot languages shift with every new wave of arrivals.

These days, the avenue is mostly a humble jumble of commercial American vernacular. Way back when, in the Gilded Age, a Kansas City pastor named George Hamilton Combs painted this picture of one of its more prominent stretches: "(It was) dressed up in high collar, white tails only from Woodland to Benton; (and) had on either side the most beturreted, the most becolored – harsh reds and oranges and purples – 'art windowed,' the most be-porticoed and scrolled 'mansions' that any American city's street ever boasted."

INTERNATIONAL STYLE

The design aesthetic from the 1920s and '30s embraced sleek, simple geometries, minimal ornament, white walls of concrete or stucco and glass. Architects associated with the German Bauhaus movement were leading proponents. In Kansas City, architect Edward Tanner built this prime example for the Walter Bixby family on State Line Road at 65th Street, in 1937. The style is often referred to as art moderne, which feels just right when you see the Bixby entry hall's Lalique staircase and lighting fixture.

I-BEAM

An I-beam is a structural metal element whose cross-section looks like its namesake letter. Pictured: Exposed and newly painted I beams in the Kansas City Ballet's Bolender Center for Dance and Creativity, which opened in 2011.

I

ITALIAN RENAISSANCE REVIVAL
Referencing materials, forms and decorative touches found in northern Italy, Italianate buildings in the area include The Kansas City Star's headquarters, (above) at 18th Street and Grand Boulevard, which opened in 1911. Architect Jarvis Hunt worked under the influence of The Star's publisher, William Rockhill Nelson, who wanted a building patterned after a historic home near Washington, D.C. A more modern example of the style with a similar square tower, stands in midtown, just off Broadway (left).

E. FAY JONES

A disciple of Frank Lloyd Wright and Oklahoman Bruce Goff, Jones (1921-2004) trained at Wright's Taliesin West and settled in Arkansas, where he long taught at the university in Fayetteville. His Thorncrown Chapel (1980) in Eureka Springs vaulted Jones to national renown and inspired a commission to build a similar expression of "Ozark Gothic," as he once put it, at Powell Gardens southeast of Kansas City.

J

HUGH NEWELL JACOBSEN

When banker James Kemper wanted to build a new house on a large, sloping site west of Ward Parkway, he turned to this prominent Washington-based modernist, who's known for a stark white look, simple geometries and tall chimneys. The house, built in 1972, comprises a series of connected pavilions, as if to suggest a village. Numerous skylights and glass-enclosed inner courtyards help bring natural light indoors.

JANSSEN PLACE

More than 100 years ago, some of the city's most prominent businessmen began building a restricted, upper-class community of stately homes along a boulevard south of 36th Street. Among the original developers was Arthur E. Stilwell, whose railroad and real estate lineage extends today to Kansas City Southern and DST. The nationally listed historic district, in the neighborhood east of Hyde Park, includes at least 19 mansions and nine carriage houses of architectural significance. The limestone, columned entry gate, currently in need of some repair, dates to 1897.

JUDGE LOUIS R. GATES HOUSE

Architect Clarence E. Shepard designed this Prairie School beauty in 1922 for a prominent civic leader of Rosedale and Wyandotte County. The stone piers, horizontal lines and narrow vertical windows, side-entry porch, slightly cantilevered second-floor windows, low and long hip roof—all add up to classic, Frank Lloyd Wright-inspired Prairie design. Shepard (1869-1949) indeed worked as a draftsman for Wright before arriving in Kansas City in 1905. The Gates residence stands in the Hanover Heights Historic District, south of the University of Kansas Medical Center. It's one of more than 600 houses Shepard designed, many of them for the J.C. Nichols Co.

JAZZ

Charlie "Bird" Parker, memorialized in this public sculpture by Robert Graham, remains one of the most significant symbols of Kansas City's musical heritage. The sculpture, dedicated in 1999, stands in park space near 18th and Vine. Despite the fact that the downtown skyline can be seen over Bird's imaginary shoulder, the designated jazz district and onetime thriving center of black Kansas City has been redeveloped only in fits and starts over the last quarter century. With the Mutual Musicians Foundation (one of the nation's great bars, according to Playboy magazine), the American Jazz Museum, a couple of viable eateries and clubs, the district deserves more love and attention from locals, funders and tourists alike.

JOLT

Two recent preservation battles got the Historic Kansas City Foundation fired up and taking action. Round one: This late 19th-century commercial building (left), the former Cosby Hotel at Ninth Street and Baltimore Avenue, was threatened with city-ordered demolition in 2010. A compromise effort to save the building made some progress, but the building's owner pulled the plug on a possible deal. Or maybe not. In the summer of 2011, new developers stepped forward to buy and rehab the building. Round two: Country Club Plaza developer Highwoods Properties and law firm Polsinelli Shughart announced a new office building (and another historic demolition) on a prominent corner, leading to outcry, compromise and uncertainty. The Balcony Building (mid-1920s), with such decorative touches as this eye-level figurative capital, survived and the office project proposal eventually was withdrawn.

JENSEN-SALSBERY BUILDING Kansas City architect Ernest O. Brostrom (1888-1969) had such a strong interest in following the lead of the Prairie School architects that he tried—unsuccessfully—to get a job working for Frank Lloyd Wright. His design for this veterinary medicine laboratory, completed in 1919, reflected the Midwestern movement's emphasis on strong horizontal lines. As Donald Hoffmann, The Kansas City Star's former architecture critic, wrote in 1964, Brostrom "had a romantic sensibility and he had the discrimination to see, in those early years of the century, the great hopes for a truly American architecture." Now known as the McQueeny Lock Co., at 520 West Pennway, the building houses various commercial operations. Brostrom hired Jorgen C. Dreyer, a Norwegian immigrant, to create the third-story sculptures, another nod to the Prairie School's interest in mixing architecture and art.

J

K

KEMPER ARENA

White elephant or historic architecture of the future? This civic project in the former cattle precincts of the West Bottoms opened in 1974 after labor strikes and other delays. Designed by Helmut Jahn of the Chicago firm C.F. Murphy Associates and constructed for $23.5 million, the building, with its distinctive exoskeletal structure, won a national honor award from the American Institute of Architects in 1976. Home of the American Royal and the 1976 GOP presidential convention, it suffered the indignity of a roof collapse during a wind and rainstorm in 1979. Nearly three decades later, indignity arrived again in the form of a new downtown arena, the Sprint Center, which has made Kemper's viability uncertain.

KEMPER MUSEUM OF CONTEMPORARY ART

Architect Gunnar Birkerts designed the low-lying, winged scheme of this contemporary art museum, which opened in 1994.

LOUIS KAHN

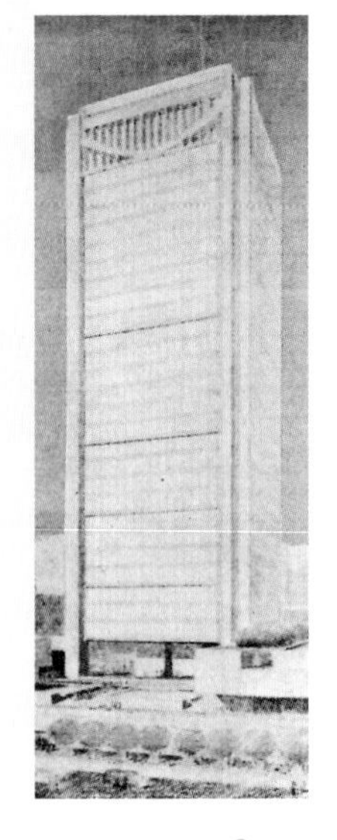

In 1972, after several years in the making, the esteemed Philadelphia-based architect (1901-1974) delivered a design for his first commercial skyscraper. The plan would have it towering above the high-profile intersection of 12th and Main streets. Oops. Kahn, creator of such revered works of architecture as the Kimbell Art Museum (1972) and the Salk Institute (1965), proposed a rather radical way of building the 32-story tower. Office floors would hang from large trusses at the building crown, and essentially the tower would have been built (efficiently and quickly, in retrospect) from the top down.

Developers (and especially their lenders) got cold feet and rejected the plan. In stepped the Chicago firm of Skidmore Owings & Merrill, and after numerous delays, the precast-lined City Center Square opened for business in 1977. An alphabetical bonus: Kahn's structural engineer on the project was August E. Komendant.

KELLY'S

Though it might feel like something out of the 19th century, this popular Westport watering hole came along much later. But it does operate in a building that began life in 1851 as Albert Gallatin Boone's trading post. It has long been considered the oldest commercial structure in town, as well as the oldest brick building.

KATZ HALL

The prominent and influential firm of Kivett & Myers designed this assertively 1960s building on the University of Missouri-Kansas City Volker campus to house the pharmacy school. After renovations in the summer of 2010, the university's Department of Architecture, Urban Planning and Design moved in, taking advantage of the building's airy, open spaces. Among other attractive features, even the stairways are daylighted. As for Kivett (named for firm founder Clarence Kivett and his longtime partner Ralph Myers Sr.), its place-defining projects include Kansas City International Airport and the Truman Sports Complex; it later merged with HNTB and the alumni have populated architectural firms all over town.

SELBY KURFISS

It's a little hard to imagine that one person is responsible for these two structures: a fine Arts and Crafts residence in Brookside dating to 1915, and the straightforward brick commercial building, originally built for a bakery in 1910, which has long housed one of Kansas City's best-known barbecue institutions, Arthur Bryant's. But Selby Kurfiss (d. 1949), an architect best known for numerous stately houses in some of Kansas City's finest neighborhoods, did, indeed, produce them both.

Kurfiss was a Kentucky native. By 1891 he was working in Kansas City as a draftsman for Adriance Van Brunt. He struck out on his own for most of the early decades of the 20th century. During the World War II years, he did military-related architectural work. Among other accomplishments, he invented a floating airfield.

KANSAS CITY LIFE INSURANCE CO.

A decade before the firm of Wight & Wight realized its neoclassical design for the Nelson-Atkins Museum of Art, it designed this beaux-arts office building (1924) for the Kansas City Life Insurance Co., at 3520 Broadway. Creator of the lioness sculpture was Jorgen C. Dreyer, the aforementioned Norwegian immigrant who created the human figures on the old Jensen-Salsbery Building.

GEORGE E. KESSLER
Kessler (1862-1923), a landscape architect, was the man most responsible for shaping Kansas City's parks and boulevard system. He was interested in and clearly influenced by the work of the famed Frederick Law Olmsted, designer of New York's Central Park. Kessler arrived here in the 1880s and designed Hyde Park. In 1893 he presented a plan for a winding system of green spaces and roadways that not only transformed Kansas City then and well into the future but helped prompt a nationwide City Beautiful Movement. North Terrace Park, in the city's northeast district, was later renamed in his honor. And its beaux-arts colonnade, built in 1908 off Gladstone Boulevard, is one of his landmark legacies.

K

LENS

Architect Steven Holl introduced a whole new language onto the Kansas City landscape when he envisioned the expansion of the Nelson-Atkins Museum of Art. The plan included a series of glass-walled pavilions, which, thinking about the transmission and diffraction of light, Holl called "lenses." Some locals came up with other names for the structures, but that's how it goes. On the inside, the lenses help give visitors ever-changing encounters with light.

L

LOOMIS HOUSE

This Italianate farmhouse at 8325 Johnson Dr. dates to 1886 and anchors the Loomis Historic District of Merriam. Original settler Emily Loomis paid $10,000 for a quarter section of land a few years earlier. Other nearby pieces of the district include a Craftsman bungalow built in 1912 by her son; a World War II-era "minimal traditional" house; and a Quaker Mission shed said to date to 1840.

LIQUID CARBONIC CO. BUILDING

Thousands of First Friday strollers each month pass this high-visibility Crossroads Arts District building at 2000 Baltimore Ave., but few probably realize what contribution it made to good times of yore. Liquid Carbonic, you see, was "The Greatest Soda Water Supply House in the World," and a branch of the Chicago-based company landed in this building when it was erected in 1913. It supplied soda fountains and later produced dry ice. The company moved to the West Bottoms in 1935. The building remains a classic reminder of the commercial and warehouse activity that characterized the neighborhood for much of the 20th century.

LUZIER COSMETICS CO. BUILDING

This exquisitely adorned building, from 1928, escaped total demolition during the development of the adjacent Midtown Marketplace (Costco, Home Depot and big asphalt parking lots) off Linwood Boulevard. Nevertheless, it remains a mere shell of its original form—and an increasingly decaying one, at that. The architectural legacy of Nelle E. Peters will shrink further if the privately owned Luzier site, at 3216 Gillham Rd., is allowed to rot away. Historian George Ehrlich called the structure's façade "one of her most effective designs."

LOOSE PARK

Site of the three-day Battle of Westport in October 1864, this much-adored urban green space was once envisioned by local civic leaders as a national park memorializing the Civil War. Instead, developer J.C. Nichols enticed Mrs. Jacob A. Loose to buy the property in 1927 (for $500,000) and give it to the city as a memorial to her late husband, a philanthropist and chairman of the Loose-Wiles Biscuit Co. Of course, it also enhanced Nichols' surrounding residential developments. As a work of landscape architecture, the park combines formal features (the Rose Garden and shelter house) and man-made walkways, a duck pond and stone walls with seemingly natural arrays of open lawns and wooded groves. For joggers, dog walkers, Frisbee-throwers and countless wedding parties—priceless.

LIMESTONE

Kansas City is shaped fundamentally by limestone outcroppings and the bedrock remnants of the inland ocean that date to millions of years ago. When industrial-age builders arrived, they smartly and conveniently used resources at hand, and, from the late 19th-century onward, limestone walls and foundations proliferated. Stone exteriors, either rustically rough or finely dressed, symbolize prosperity (homes), solidity (churches and civic buildings) or both (banks and other commercial structures). "Limestone is timeless as a building material," says Richard Wetzel, a Kansas City architect and builder. "It's durable, beautiful and local." And, he adds, it's heavy and expensive.

Limestone, whether native or imported, can be found expressing natural values in some of the most prominent Kansas City buildings. Some lesser known stone sites worth noticing include these:

- In Kansas City, Kan., in 1938, architect Raymond Buschhusen created a tapestry of limestone for the now-historic Dr. A. Porter Davis home, known as Castle Rock, at Ninth Street and Washington Boulevard (left).

- The fate is uncertain for the limestone-clad Wheatley-Provident Hospital, (below) built in 1908 as the St. Joseph Parochial School, 1826 Forest Ave. In 1917, the original Collegiate Gothic building (architect unknown) became the city's first hospital operated by and for African-Americans. A mid-1920s addition was designed by the prominent firm of Hoit, Price & Barnes. The

vacant structure, owned privately, was placed on the Kansas City Historic Register in 2007. The Wheatley deserves historic status if only for a tragic memory: It's where notable young bandleader Bennie Moten died during surgery in 1935. The Missouri Alliance for Historic Preservation has listed the building as one of the state's most endangered historic properties.

• Fieldstone corner pillars frame the former Fire Station No. 28 at 5947 Troost Ave. (above and left), and contrasting stone slabs highlight the façade above the entry. The building dates to 1911 and was designed by the increasingly interesting architect Edgar C. Faris, whose work also appears in a few Mediterranean-inspired structures in midtown KC.

L

R.A. LONG BUILDING

When it opened as the headquarters of the Long-Bell Lumber Co. in 1906, this Renaissance Revival skyscraper, on the northwest corner of 10th Street and Grand Avenue, represented the pinnacle of Kansas City business ambition and power. R.A. Long spared no expense. Aided by architect Henry Hoit, Long poured $1.4 million into the 14-story structure, which boasted six high-speed elevators and all the finest features of the day. The building now houses operations of UMB Bank.

MAST HEADQUARTERS

Long before the current discussion of what to do with vacant big-box retail stores, in 1997 the local firm of Shaughnessy Fickel & Scott transformed a former Kmart store on Eastwood Trafficway into an expanded home for the local ambulance service, now part of the Kansas City Fire Department. The one story structure includes garage, dispatch center, auditorium, classrooms and offices in a colorful interior.

MURAL

When the owner of a few buildings on Southwest Boulevard at Broadway wanted to put an end to incessant graffiti, he turned to street artist Scribe to create a series of vibrant, surreal scenes on several exterior walls. In a way it's an example of privately funded public art and also the kind of small, serendipitous urban moment that contributes to a city's uniqueness.

LUDWIG MIES VAN DER ROHE
The Chicago office of this vaunted 20th century German-American architect (1886-1969) produced this steel and glass office tower for Crown Center in 1977. It's typical of the modernism Mies promoted with his "less is more" philosophy.

MARBURG
That was the name of the lavish, perhaps German-inspired home of August R. Meyer, a business tycoon, engineer and first park board president, built in 1896-97 at 4415 Warwick Blvd. Now, it's known as Vanderslice Hall, the administration building of the Kansas City Art Institute. The firm of Van Brunt & Howe designed the original rambling three-story mansion. Architects Wight & Wight, also known for the Nelson-Atkins Museum of Art nearby, also had a hand in expanding it when the Art Institute moved in, in 1928. As for Meyer, we also remember him locally with a boulevard, a fountain and a monument.

MUTUAL MUSICIANS FOUNDATION
Built in 1904 as an apartment building, this simple brick, concrete and stucco structure became the home of the black musicians union in 1928. Its walls have absorbed the sounds of all the great musicians of the city's jazz heyday: Count Basie, Bennie Moten, Jay McShann, Charlie Parker and more. The Foundation, one of the last original, intact vestiges of the historic 18th and Vine District, remains alive today with late-night weekend jam sessions. A long-idle effort to rehab and preserve an adjacent hotel and a group of modest houses across the street was poised to resume in 2011.

JOHN W. MCKECKNIE

This Ohio native, a product of Princeton and Columbia universities, arrived in Kansas City in the late 1890s and went on to put his architectural stamp on our town over the next four decades (he died in 1934 at age 72). He designed more than 120 commercial buildings and high-toned residences here, many of them reflecting a special eye for detail and distinctiveness. Architectural historian George Ehrlich said of McKecknie: "(He) can be taken as representative of the better designers of his generation."

McKecknie is often recognized as a pioneer in the use of reinforced concrete, a material advancement of the late 19th century. His Gumbel Building of 1904, at 801 Walnut St., (see page 41) was an early example, as was the 12-story Gloyd Building/Columbia National Bank, which is considered the first reinforced-concrete skyscraper in town. Sadly, the latter was demolished in 2002 to make way for a parking garage.

In 1908, McKechnie designed a warehouse for Montgomery Ward at

19th and Campbell streets, then doubled its size two years later. The horizontal banding of the exterior (opposite left) was typical of McKecknie's standout design touches, as were the brawny concrete columns inside. Montgomery Ward moved its operation to 6220 St. John Ave. (1913), another huge and utilitarian facility of McKecknie's design, and the first building became home to what is now known as Tension Envelope.

McKecknie also designed the Grand Avenue Temple (1912) and its adjacent office tower and the University Club (1922-23). He is also credited with a group of colonnaded apartment buildings on Armour Boulevard, between Baltimore and Wyandotte, which have historic interest as residences in a Kansas City vernacular. Some of those buildings stand vacant awaiting possible renovation (right). Among McKecknie's notable residences are the Calvert Hunt home on Gladstone Boulevard (1904, opposite top and bottom) and an art nouveau-inspired brick and stone house at 720 E. 36th St. in Hyde Park (1906, top).

LEWIS MUMFORD
We can thank this historian and longtime architecture critic (1895-1990) for giving us much-needed insights such as this: "Forget the damned motor car and build the cities for lovers and friends."

M

NEW ORLEANS
Reconstruction of the Crescent City, even six years after the devastation wrought by Hurricane Katrina, continues to pose some of the toughest questions about urban development, planning, design, home building, environment and community this nation has ever faced. In addition to the celebrity glamour of Brad Pitt, who grew up in Missouri, Kansas Citians are well represented in the rebuilding effort. Architects from BNIM and Gould Evans are among those involved in New Orleans projects. Pictured: BNIM design for a "Make It Right" duplex in New Orleans.

n

NEWBERN APARTMENTS
The elaborate terra-cotta arch above the main entrance contributes to this Armour Boulevard building's association with the Sullivanesque style. Built in the early 1920s and opened as the Peacock Hotel, the structure was designed by architect Ernest O. Brostrom and originally bore six-foot ornamental peacocks above its north and east entrances. In 1925, Brostrom's arch design replaced the peacocks, which apparently were a turnoff for potential hotel guests.

HOMER F. NEVILLE

Yes, our city was shaped profoundly by men named Nichols and Nelson, but we pause now to recognize instead a lesser-known builder. Homer F. Neville (1900-1991) was an architect whose portfolio included Kansas City's Municipal Auditorium (1935), the original Midwest Research Institute (1953) and (Jayhawkers, take note) the campanile or carillon tower (1951, with Edward B. Delk) on the University of Kansas campus in Lawrence. (He was a product of its architecture program.) In 1966, Neville, hired to return to Municipal Auditorium and update the interior, got into a public spat with the Municipal Art Commission. The commission rejected the contemporary, metallic wall-coverings he had picked out and opted for quieter, reddish-brown tones. "I think this terra-cotta on the walls is a tragedy," he told The Star at the time. Do architects and bureaucrats ever get along?

NEON

Bright lights, big city. Well, maybe in Tokyo or Vegas or New York. But perhaps Kansas City, a dimmer place, can have its neon moments, too. Neon lighting sparks a sense of urban flash, chaos and no small amount of nostalgia. As LED technology and monster video billboards muscle their way onto landscapes everywhere, it's comforting to hold on to the colorful, tubular signs of old, which liven our streetscapes and light up our lives.

NICHOLSON RESIDENCE

From the architects who gave us the original Nelson-Atkins Museum of Art, City Hall and downtown's Jackson County Courthouse comes this assertively Neo-Classical home near Ward Parkway. The firm of Wight and Wight produced only a handful of residences in Kansas City. This one, at 1028 W. 58th St., was built in 1917-18 for zinc-mine baron George E. Nicholson. The design adheres to principals of the Corinthian Order as evidenced by the tetrastyle, or four-column front, and other details. Another prominent firm, the landscape architects Hare and Hare, laid out the grounds around the home.

NEW ENGLAND BUILDING

This sturdy survivor, at 122 W. Ninth St., is one of the last of a breed of great commercial buildings dating to the city's building boom of the late 1880s. Befitting its name and East Coast developers, it was designed by a Boston architectural firm. Stone foundation walls are three feet thick. The sandstone exterior remains alive with carved ornamental details such as those on this distinctive two-story bay window. Like its better-known neighbor to the east, the eagle-bearing New York Life Building (above, designed by the hallowed firm of McKim Mead & White), the New England Building reflects its era's interest in Renaissance Revival architecture. More alphabetical relevance: The buildings are in the Ninth Street Historic District.

NEW URBANISM

This modern movement in real estate development attempts to urbanize suburbia by building walkable shopping districts, such as the Northland's Zona Rosa, in the midst of vibrant residential settings. The granddaddy vision of all that came from J.C. Nichols and the Country Club Plaza. So far, it seems, in the modern suburban version of new urbanism, the shopping dominates and the ideal of real mixed-use, pedestrian-oriented living remains mostly elusive. In the future, city planners may stress another kind of "new urbanism" —one that will promote the anti-sprawl idea of reinvigorating core cities with denser, infill and human-scale mixed-use developments.

NORTH PATROL DIVISION

From its hillside perch, the safety-yellow police station off U.S. 169 and Barry Road has been an unmissable presence since it opened in 1978. But there's a general sense it performed better as architecture (from the firm of Devine James Labinski Myers) than as a police station. Now its days are numbered. The Kansas City Police Department has been upgrading and building new facilities for the last decade, and a recent sales-tax extension is likely to result in a replacement building for North Patrol.

OLYMPIC STADIUM

Well, we can dream about holding the Olympics in Kansas City, probably long after my lifetime, but our town does have a connection to the 2012 Summer Games in London. The sports architecture firm Populous designed the main stadium and other details of the 2012 Olympic park, which I photographed in 2010 while it was under construction on the east side of London. The stadium will be surrounded by an array of twisted fabric panels, colorfully lighted at night.

OASIS

Literally, it's a pool of water in the desert, but figuratively, it's any relief from dullness. So an office building's backyard pool, accompanied by landscaping and benches, certainly qualifies. This one appears behind the UMB Bank Building at 4900 Main St. Kansas City probably has countless surprising places and unexpected opportunities for quiet respite from the daily grind and relentless bland.

ORANGE

Splashes of bright color command attention, which is why highway barrels and snow fences typically come in safety orange. The architects at Helix made a dramatic gesture when they gave this Main Street garage a bold orange stripe. The effect was partly in response to the red-paneled windows at the old, now renovated, TWA headquarters next door. It's fair to note that the colors of those two buildings sometimes seem to clash more than they complement each other. Still, the Helix inspiration came directly from the color of safety cones, says the firm's Bryan Gross. The orange works to differentiate between the car-oriented space above and the pedestrian, retail activity on the ground. And, he says, "It cradles and protects that zone where people come down the stairs."

ONE KANSAS CITY PLACE

Driving north on Main Street, you can get your first glimpse of this downtown skyscraper as you crest the hill at 45th Street just up from the Country Club Plaza. The tower pops into view straight ahead like a distant wonder, gray and beguiling and perhaps, in the traveler's imagination, the seat of all-knowing power. Downtown's most prominent office building, at 42 stories, is a sleek, faceted sculpture in glass, albeit one that has been long considered too understated for its own good (and ours). Yet after more than 20 years in the skyline (it opened in 1988), the building, designed by the firm now known as BNIM, speaks with a kind of pin-striped elegance. In a skyline beauty contest, that gives it an edge over its neighbors of the same generation, the more overtly postmodern Town Pavilion (reflected in this photo) and 1201 Walnut.

OLD LEAWOOD

With its wooded, rolling terrain, the northern stretch of Leawood (roughly Somerset Drive to 95th Street, State Line Road to Mission Road) made for an idyllic inner-ring suburb, complete with rambling ranch-style homes and restrictive covenants. Nowadays, some older sections of the city, which were incorporated in 1948, are being made new again by homeowners wanting larger, more up-to-date places to live. A preservation movement has been established to combat out-of-place McMansions in Old Leawood. Still, pockets of modernity have emerged. Architect Matthew Hufft eschewed the hide-the-addition approach when clients had him design this sleek, modern expansion and renovation (2009) of a typical Leawood ranch.

ORNAMENT 

The depiction of heroes and allegories on civic structures surely dates to the Parthenon and beyond. The impulse to decorate buildings was wrung out of the language of architecture by 20th-century modernism. Still, monuments remain. And this example of public ornamentation can be seen on the west facade of the downtown Jackson County Courthouse (1934). It and three others on the building were carved by Charles L. Keck (1875-1951), a widely employed sculptor and monument maker, who also created the bronze statue of Andrew Jackson around the corner. Keck's work also can be seen in narrative panels on the exterior of the Nelson-Atkins Museum of Art.

p

PRESCOTT PASSIVE HOUSE
This recently completed home at 32 S. 16th St., Kansas City, Kan., is another in a series of cutting-edge residential projects built by architecture students in the Studio 804 program at the University of Kansas. Under the guidance of Dan Rockhill, the students design and build environmentally conscious homes, which, when sold, help finance the program. This three-bedroom house, in the Prescott neighborhood, achieves Passive House Certification, which means it was designed with a thicker-than-average shell and other features to reduce heating and cooling costs by 90 percent. It joins about a dozen other projects nationwide that have achieved that status since 2003.

PASEO PERGOLA
This neo-classical shaded walkway, with beams atop parallel series of Doric columns, has been a landmark along the Paseo at 10th Street since about 1899.

PACIFIC HOUSE HOTEL
Built in 1860, then rebuilt eight years later after a fire, the onetime luxury hotel (credited to architect Asa B. Cross) was renovated in 1999 and now houses offices and lofts. With a cast-iron arcade on the façade, it's one of the last authentic historic buildings in the River Market area.

POSTY CARDS

When the owners of this Kansas City greeting-card firm wanted to double the size of their facility, they set a goal to make it as sustainable as possible. With features ranging from an exterior, natural-light courtyard in the middle of the building, to recycled rainwater, to one of the largest rooftop solar-panel installations around, the urban-core project is expected to achieve a LEED Platinum rating. The parking lot includes a charging station for electric vehicles. The expansion of the existing metal-skinned Butler building (2011), to a total of 45,000 square feet, was designed by Christopher Mitchell of McHenry Shaffer Mitchell.

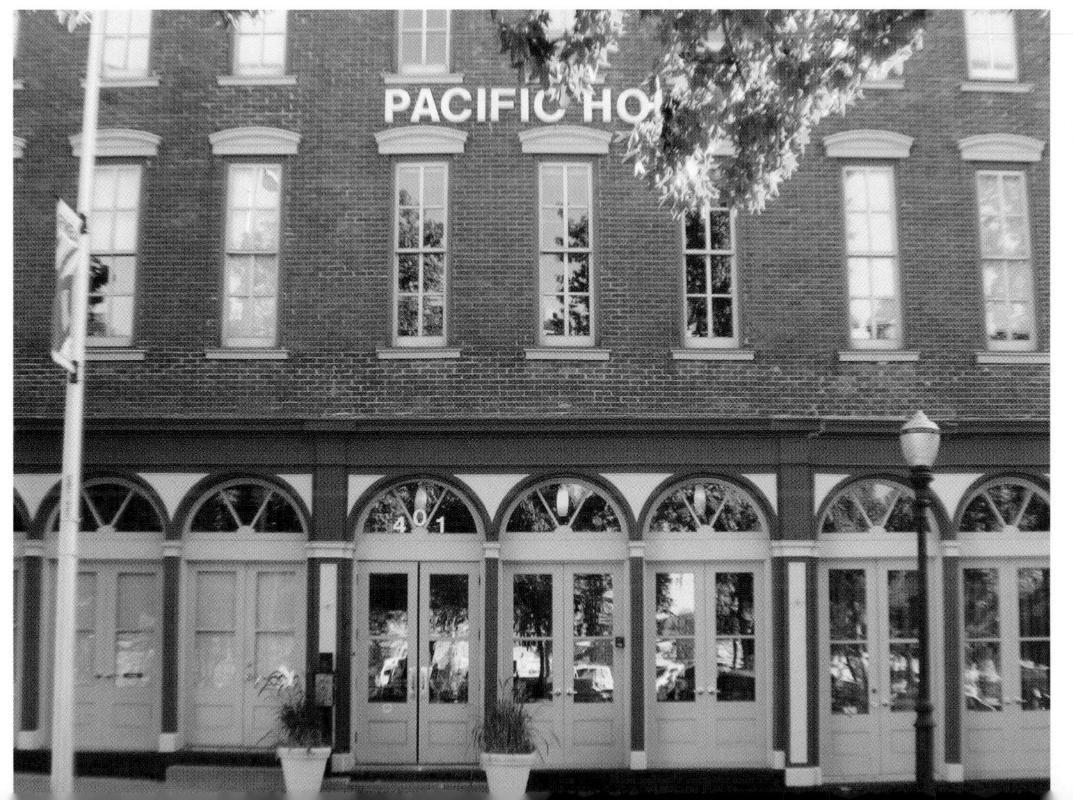

PASEO YMCA

When it was built in 1914, this branch of the Young Men's Christian Association was among the largest buildings in the predominantly black district centered on 18th and Vine streets, about a block to the east. It served as a significant social and recreational gathering place for the community. The building has been vacant since about 1970, and in recent years an effort to bring it back to life as an educational center for the Negro Leagues Baseball Museum has been trying to gain traction. The four-story brick and concrete structure retains many of its classically inspired details. Restoration of the building shell is almost complete. The derelict interior awaits.

POPULOUS

The global firm formerly known as HOK Sport Venue Event spun off from the St. Louis-based HOK Group in 2009 and gave itself an adjective for a name. Among other recent projects, the sports architecture powerhouse designed (with Rafael Architects) the expansion and renovation of Kauffman Stadium (2009). (Pictured: New meets the old in wider and more active concourses.) Its renovation of Arrowhead was completed in 2010 and the Livestrong Sporting KC soccer park opened to much acclaim in Kansas City, Kan., in 2011. Also on the boards: stadiums for the 2012 Olympics in London and for the 2014 Winter Olympics in Sochi, Russia.

PGAV

The firm of Peckham Guyton Albers Viets began in St. Louis in the mid-1960s and opened a Kansas City office four years later. It's responsible for a wide variety of local projects ranging from the redevelopment of Quality Hill in the 1980s to campus buildings and casino renovations. Among high-profile major projects are the transformation of the old Menorah Medical Center site into the Stowers Institute (2000) and Garmin International's headquarters expansion (2004) in Olathe. The Kansas Bioscience Authority's "Venture Accelerator," a 40,000-square-foot laboratory building and business incubator, opened in 2011 at Kansas 7 and College Boulevard.

PICKERING HOUSE

One of Johnson County's oldest buildings, this historic home in Olathe, dating to 1862, was undergoing restoration until the private owners ran out of funds. Its exposed state remains precarious, but city officials say they are hopeful the rescue effort can continue, and in August 2011 a new owner stepped forward to take it on. The landmark was built and expanded by a former mayor of Olathe and owned by the Pickering family for more than a century.

PLAZA CENTER BUILDING

This seven-story office building at 800 W. 47th St. was designed by the noted Chicago firm of Skidmore, Owings and Merrill and opened in 1963. The exoskeletal structure, with its pre-cast concrete bones extending beyond the glass walls, makes it a close cousin of the firm's landmark BMA Tower.

P

Q

QUEEN ANNE STYLE
This broad movement dates to the late Victorian era (1880s and '90s) but purports to look back to an earlier royal. It's often marked by rambunctious ornament and showy building features such as bay windows, towers and turrets. Examples can be seen in Hyde Park (above and upper left) and these two houses on Norledge in Northeast. Left: The work of Chicago architects Burnham and Root.

QUADRANGLE

The old quad at UMKC (above) has been elongated in recent years by campus expansion. A common feature of college campuses, the rectilinear green space is typically defined by four surrounding buildings. Rockhurst University's quadrangle (below) is bounded on one side by a pergola, tower and parking lots. College quadrangles, with their landscaped walkways, are intended mostly to impose order on the lives of undergrads who are poised mostly to resist such things.

QUALITY HILL

The term might have been ironic since it came from Confederate sympathizers who were describing the lifestyles of silk-stocking Republicans who populated this fashionable, bluff-top neighborhood as early as the 1850s. But the name stuck. After periods of posh building and decline, a development project in the 1970s injected hundreds of new housing units and helped shore up the fortunes of this historic area, roughly 10 downtown blocks west of Broadway. Most of the oldest structures date from 1856 to 1929. Residences and commercial buildings in the neighborhood, many no longer with us, were associated with some of the great names in Kansas City architecture, including Louis Curtiss, Nelle E. Peters, Ernest Brostrom and Henry Van Brunt.

A. QUINCY JONES

This Kansas City native (1913-1979) set up private practice in Los Angeles in the late 1930s and became associated with the airy, box-bending California style of residential architecture after World War II. Some of his 1950s and '60s residential design work (with partner Frederick Emmons) ended up in suburban Kansas City homes built by Donald Drummond, a California transplant to the area. One of those is this house at 9840 Aberdeen Dr., Leawood. Jones became a professor of architecture at the University of Southern California and expanded his reputation with numerous campus and office buildings in Los Angeles and beyond.

QUOIN

The term refers to often syncopated lines of exterior stones or masonry at the edge of a building that contrast in one or more ways (material, color, texture, etc.) with the rest of the wall. Pictured: The upper story of the Folly Theater – it opened as the Standard in 1900 – features quoins of goldish brick.

QUE SERA SERA
Many people point to the 39th Street commercial district in Kansas City's West Volker neighborhood as a good example of relatively unplanned, organic development. Shops, restaurants and bars have made for a lively and wildly eclectic entertainment district without the use of tax incentives and forced uniformity of design.

QUINDARO
Ruins of 28 buildings on 160 acres mark the river bluff site of this abolitionist settlement, dating to the Civil War era, in Wyandotte County. Quindaro served as an important stop on the Underground Railroad, shepherding and sheltering runaway slaves as they slipped into the free state of Kansas. A grass-roots effort began in the 1980s to save the historic site from a landfill expansion, and a new stonework overlook was dedicated in 2008. Pictured: In 2005, stonemasons worked to stabilize the foundations of the Quindaro ruins, including a hotel and other commercial buildings.

Q

R

ROANOKE PARK

This wooded ravine posed too many building challenges to developers of the surrounding residential area, so about 37 acres ended up in the hands of the Parks Department in the early years of the 20th century. The park dates to a city ordinance of 1909. This stone arch leads to a staircase on the west side of the park, off a little street called Park Court.

ELPIDIO ROCHA

His footprint here isn't large, but it wasn't for lack of trying. Rocha (circa 1971) once built an imaginative neighborhood park with a fellow Kansas City Art Institute professor, Dale Eldred. It soon gave way to Interstate 35, which sliced through the powerless West Side. Rocha designed this unconventional, Bruce Goff-inspired house for a friend in the late 1960s, and it still stands on a narrow lot on a dead-end block just west of the highway. He also designed some small parks and shelters on both sides of the state line. But his local crowning achievement was the Center City Mall, a forward-thinking, sculptural streetscape that was meant to enliven two dead blocks of Minnesota Avenue in downtown Kansas City, Kan., in the early 1970s. With its pedestrian-oriented urban plan and large fountain of stainless-steel pylons (Eldred again), the project, of course, was too radically ahead of its time and far too unpopular with locals, so it was dismantled and demolished within a few years. By then Rocha was long gone, continuing his teaching career in California and Oregon. He long championed the art, architecture and voices of Hispanic culture. "Buildings are a minor part of architecture," he once said, arguing instead for democratically inspired public spaces, "a people's architecture."

RAPHAEL HOTEL

In 1928 architect Alonzo Gentry designed the luxury Villa Serena apartments in the Italian Renaissance Revival style. The nine-story building stood along the south bank of Brush Creek, just across from the newly developed Country Club Plaza. Almost 50 years later, the J.C. Nichols Co., the Plaza developer, acquired and then converted the residential tower into a boutique hotel. And 30 years after that, in 2005, a new owner, Lighthouse Properties of Salina, Kan., began to renovate the Raphael. A makeover of the mahogany-ceiling lobby was completed in 2011.

JOSEPH W. RADOTINSKY

The son of Hungarian immigrants, Radotinsky (1902-1983) served as Kansas state architect under three governors (in the 1930s) and designed some of the most enduring buildings in Wyandotte County. Among his projects: five high schools (Argentine, Sumner, Turner, Washington and Wyandotte), the Memorial Hall auditorium (1935-37), the Kansas City, Kan., Public Library and Board of Education (1965) and the Agricultural Hall of Fame (1965). He planned school buildings and hospitals throughout the Midwest. On the Missouri side of the metro area, he designed the American Hereford Association building (now HNTB headquarters), a 1951 building (pictured), which historian George Ehrlich applauded as "a clear break from the masonry conservatism of many post-war buildings." Radotinsky owned a Hereford ranch in Wyandotte County, and, in a curious bit of history, in 1962 he was bound and gagged at the farmhouse by three prison escapees from Leavenworth who had holed up there.

J.C. ROGERS

A banker and dreamer from Wamego, Kan., Rogers (d. 1913) is best known for buying several buildings from the World's Columbian Exposition in 1893 in Chicago and rebuilding or storing their pieces in Kansas City. The fair's Wisconsin Building, for example, once stood at Seventh Street and Grand Boulevard and operated as a men's club. Many artifacts Rogers bought at the fair ended up in the historic Columbian Theater in Wamego.

RIVER MARKET REDEVELOPMENT

The revival of downtown living might be dated to 1997-98, when two warehouse conversions—River Bend (below) and Richards & Conover—helped kick-start a residential movement between the Missouri River and the central business district. Both loft projects were much aided by state and federal historic tax credits.

ROW HOUSES

Often cited as a rare remaining example of the form, these attached houses at 34th and Main streets went up in 1887-88 during one of the city's great building booms. The bays, contrasting textures of brick and limestone and asymmetrical arrays of other details put the buildings squarely in the Queen Anne style.

R

RICE-TREMONTI HOUSE
This Gothic Revival farmhouse at 8801 E. 66th St., Raytown, said to be the oldest extant frame house in Jackson County, dates to the 1840s. It served as a way station on the Santa Fe, Oregon and California trails. For the last two decades, the home has been operated as a museum by a preservation group ever in search of upkeep funds: www.rice-tremonti.com.

SONDERN-ADLER HOUSE

One of two Kansas City houses designed by Frank Lloyd Wright, this ground-hugging Roanoke neighborhood landmark, at 3600 Belleview Ave., was built in 1940 for Clarence W. Sondern. The small house reflected Wright's ideally practical Usonian concept. It was an L-shaped structure with concrete slab floors embedded with steam pipes for radiant heating. Ten years later, a subsequent owner, Arnold Adler, added a larger living room under Wright's direction. The interior offers wide views of the outdoors. The woodwork is almost entirely cypress.

ST. TERESA'S ACADEMY

As the school migrated from downtown to 57th and Main streets, its Music and Arts Building was built in 1909. The local firm of Wilder & Wight devised the red brick building's restrained and tasteful neoclassic style. The building features an egg-shaped auditorium with austere Roman arches and a quiet expanse of white plaster inset with an art-glass dome. (An exterior covering was added in 1988 to prevent further leaking.) The auditorium gained an early reputation for high-level acoustics.

SUNSET DRIVE OFFICE BUILDING

Several Johnson County government agencies operate out of this Olathe facility, one of the greenest buildings in the metro area. The $30 million energy-saving building, designed by 360 Architecture, opened in 2006 and incorporates a long list of environmentally sensitive features ranging from gray-water recycling and stormwater-capturing bioswales to extensive daylighting and recyclable furnishing fabrics made from corn.

SOLAR SHELTER

The more you think about it, the more you'd conclude that a city park is a natural, ready-made solar-powered environment. But progress must be made and in 2010, during a renovation of Westwood Park at 47th Street and State Line Road, this solar-powered picnic shelter was born. Similar installations have been installed or are in the works for the alphabetically appropriate Spring Valley and Sunnyside parks. And the Parks Department operates solar-powered fountains at Meyer Boulevard and the Paseo and the Swope Memorial golf course.

SPILLWAY AND DAM

When the city of Lenexa and the engineering firm Black & Veatch envisioned a new stormwater project a few years back, they recast it from routine infrastructure to a visible, usable public asset. The result: Lake Lenexa, a 35-acre recreational body of water plus streamways, trails and other natural accoutrements at Black Hoof Park. With its curvy lines, patterned stairways and other design details, the dam and spillway project offers an unusual level of aesthetic achievement in such a massive, concrete civic structure. And lots of people have noticed, including the U.S. Society of Dams, which in 2009, handed it an award for excellence.

SIMPSON HOUSE

This local favorite turned 100 in 2009. An attorney named Burnett Simpson ordered up this well-appointed home in the Richardson Romanesque style. Built of limestone from Carthage, Mo., and detailed with fancy wood trim, lead crystal and stained glass, the house was acquired in the early 1980s by the All Souls Unitarian Universalist Church next door and renovated for use as an event space.

SCARRITT BUILDING, SCARRITT ARCADE

The 11-story tower, at 818 Grand Blvd., and four-story arcade, 819 Walnut St., present some fine architectural detail reflecting the ornamented influence of Louis Sullivan and the Chicago School. Built in 1907 (by architects Root and Siemens) and rehabbed (by Solomon Claybaugh Young) in 1985, the office buildings were erected by Judge Edward "Lucky" Scarritt as high-toned quarters for lawyers. Interiors are known for their open spaces, natural light and decorative details. High above Grand is the Scarritt Building's overhanging cornice. The arcade's entry façade includes two circular windows.

T

TWA BUILDING

This mid-century modern office building, built as corporate headquarters for Trans World Airlines in the mid-1950s, got a restorative boost from a developer's use of state and federal historic tax credits. Since its rehab and reopening in 2006, it's enjoying life again as the home of the Barkley advertising agency. With its planted and decked rooftop, the red and white exterior and the replica rocket, the building at 1735 Baltimore easily makes a claim as one of the most distinctive in town. The original, curtain-wall design, influenced by Mies van der Rohe, came from architects Raymond Bales Jr. and Morris Schechter.

TENSEGRITY

Kenneth Snelson's outdoor sculpture "Triple Crown," installed in 1991 at the south end of Crown Center, reflects a structural idea associated with his onetime teacher Buckminster Fuller. The word refers to the balance of tension and compression in various kinds of three-dimensional woven forms. And an exhilarating sense of balance, plus a lively marriage of art and science, is what Snelson achieves in his array of stainless steel tubes and cables.

TOWN OF KANSAS PEDESTRIAN BRIDGE

Just about anything that gets our populace closer to the city's most important but underappreciated natural asset, the Missouri River, is OK in my book. Although some commemorative projects envisioned for the site of the city's founding remain unrealized, this 635-foot-long steel and ironwood structure extends from the end of Main Street, north of Second, to a river overlook and connects to a riverfront hiking and biking trail. The $4 million project, designed by Tom Nelson of BNIM, opened in 2002.

TOWN PAVILION

Can a postmodern building improve with age? When it went up a quarter of a century ago, the tower then known as the AT&T Town Pavilion planted a kind of soul-less glass tree in the heart of a relatively quiet downtown. Today, in light of the city's urban revival, the building, designed by HNTB, might be getting a second chance for our affections. It does have its visual moments, such as this interior view to the west from the barrel-vaulted rotunda.

TOWN TOPIC

A cinder-block box. A thin brick façade. A lighted googie sign. What more does it take to make a bit of American vernacular architecture? Well, perhaps, a white picket fence along the parking lot of this old-favorite, mid-century diner at Baltimore Avenue and Southwest Boulevard. It's one of two Town Topics in the Crossroads District—simple, authentic buildings that work as planned.

TIFFANY RESIDENCE

A century ago, architect Clifford B. Sloan designed this rough-stone Tudor castle, at 100 Garfield Ave., for a prominent physician, Flavel Tiffany. Historian George Ehrlich referred to it as a "medieval fantasy." It remains one of the residential gems of the Pendleton Heights neighborhood in the Northeast district. (Historical aside: When the good Doctor Tiffany died in January 1918, his obituary in The Star was most likely reported by a budding young journalist named Ernest Hemingway.)

TIMBER

Old warehouse and industrial buildings throughout downtown Kansas City were built with bones of big timber. When the Accardo family's Broadway Development renovated this early 20th century structure at 310 W. 20th St., architect Matt Gearhart kept it simple: "All we did was sandblasted and cleaned up the existing structure and kept that natural beauty." This building dates to 1905 and housed what was then known as the Zahner Manufacturing Co.

T

TROMANHAUSER HOUSE
Louis Curtiss designed this two-bedroom Roanoke neighborhood home in 1914, mixing details and gestures from Prairie, Spanish and other styles.

TRUMAN HOME
The historic, 18-room Victorian mansion, at 219 N. Delaware, Independence, is operated by the National Park Service and underwent extensive restoration in 2009 and 2010.

U

UNIVERSITY OF KANSAS HOSPITAL

The medical center and university complex at 39th Street and Rainbow Boulevard has been expanding in recent years, to the tune of $300 million or more in new construction. Lots of glass and institutional flair have transformed the character of the campus from its buttoned-up brick origins. The Center for Advanced Heart Care (right) opened in 2006 and is now getting three more floors (RTKL of Dallas). An 183,000-square-foot medical office building (Cannon Design of St. Louis) was under construction in 2011. Bands of textured stone and glass define the north façade of the Robert E. Hemenway Life Sciences Innovation Center (below), which opened in 2007 (Cannon Design and Treanor Architects of Lawrence).

UGLY 

Or, perhaps, "unwelcoming." Hundreds of people a day use this Country Club Plaza garage, the Valencia Place entry off 47th Street. For many shoppers or tourists, it's the portal to what is supposed to be an enlivening, economically stimulating experience. Yet the long tunnel is a dreary bridge to daylight (even without the occasional black plastic rattrap near the sidewalk). It's uncomfortable for walking and hardly befitting what for many is a first impression of a place we otherwise like to tout. Long, blank walls sport not a single Spanish tile, let alone any other meaningful attempt at humanizing what is essentially a public space. Good design is in the details, and in this case the details must have given way to "value engineering," or, in layman's terms, cost cutting. So there: I've gotten a long-held complaint off my chest.

UNION CARBIDE BUILDING

This high-rise from architect William A. Bovard, at 912 Baltimore Ave., opened in 1931 at the height of the Depression as well as downtown's construction and art deco booms. Terra-cotta panels decorate the penthouse level and the east façade. Originally called the Carbide and Carbon Building, its first owner was Washington University of St. Louis. In recent years, the building has been converted to condos.

UNITARIAN FELLOWSHIP

Architects Josh Shelton and Steve Salzer at El Dorado Inc. kept the quiet Kansas landscape in mind when adding an award-winning, sleekly modern lobby and sanctuary to this church south of Lawrence. The new structure, built in 2007, totals 4,000 square feet. It sidles up to a former one-room schoolhouse, dating from the 1880s, and sits beneath a towering, century-old hedgerow, which contributes to the shading scheme.

UNION CEMETERY

This final resting place quietly houses some of the city's earliest residents—55,000 of them—in the shadow of modern office towers and urban condos. The city's oldest public burial ground, established in 1857 near 28th and Main streets, is a rolling park fringed by limestone outcroppings. It got its name because of its location, signifying a union of the separate towns of Kansas City and Westport.

UNION STATION

It has been more than 10 years since the long-ignored Union Station was brought back from the dead. Though its finances remain shaky and its future still precarious, this fact remains: It's our humongous landmark (designed by architect Jarvis Hunt), and we should learn to engage it more often and love it more than we seem to do. Here's hoping we still have it when it reaches the 100th anniversary of its opening, in 2014. Party, anyone?

U

URBAN VISION

Simmering again on a civic burner is the notion of putting a cap on the south loop highway that long ago severed downtown. A study by HNTB prompted some pre-recession City Hall enthusiasm for the project (cost: up to $180 million for a six-block area). Planners envision new public green space and potential development opportunities where the revived downtown core meets the Crossroads. (The view pictured here is west from Oak Street.) As the Chicago visionary architect and urban planner Daniel Burnham notably put it, "Make no little plans."

V

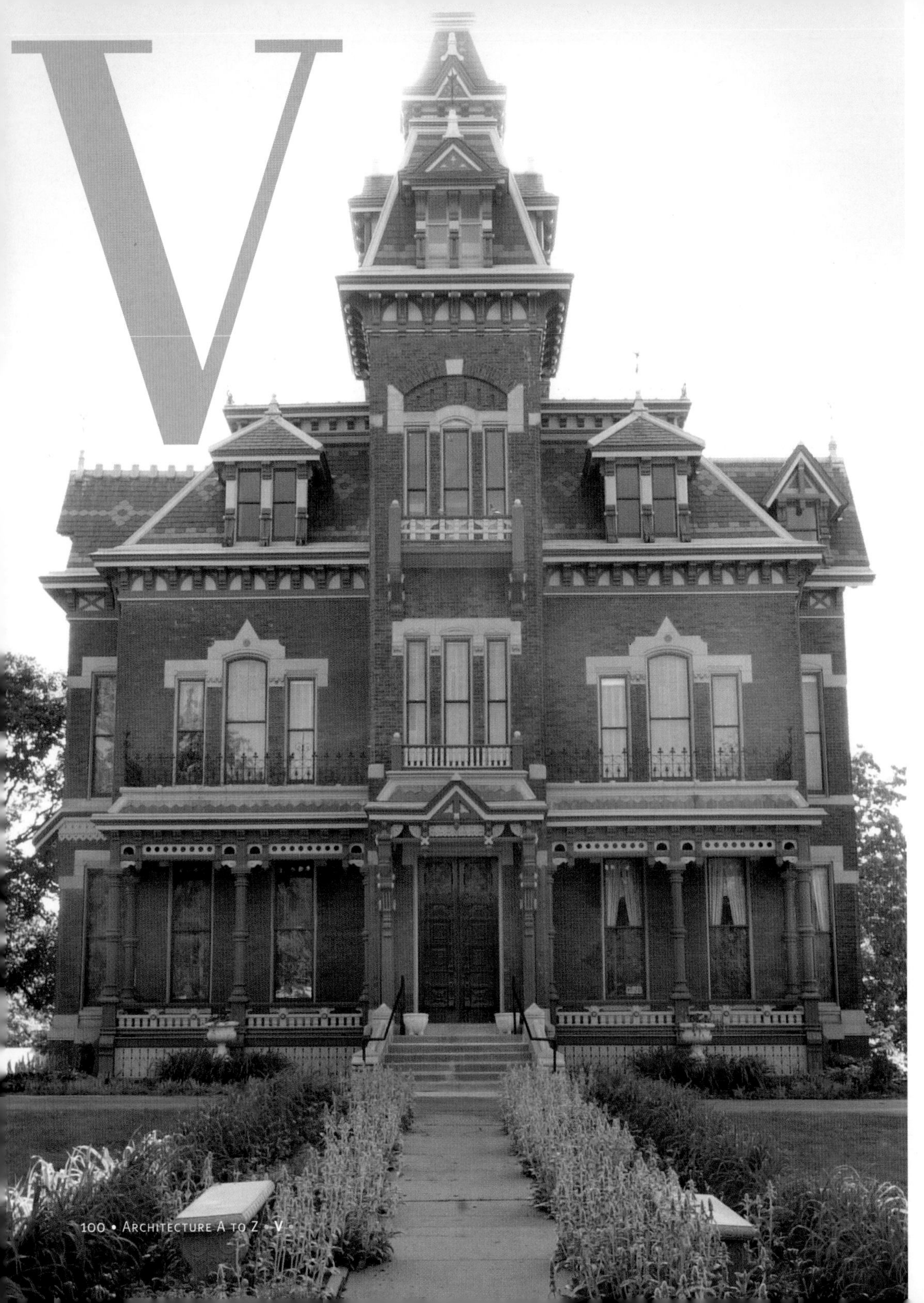

VAILE MANSION
Col. Harvey M. Vaile and his wife commissioned architect Asa Beebe Cross to make this Independence showplace befitting an influential business tycoon. (He had an interest in the construction of the Erie Canal and was acquitted on charges involving a mail route he owned.) The Second Empire bonbon, tricked-out with all manner of ornamental flourishes, reminded the couple of a house they'd visited in Normandy. They moved in in 1881. At a cost of $100,000 (more than $2 million in today's dollars), the mansion rambled through 30-odd rooms, under 14-foot-high ceilings. It boasted nine marble-trimmed fireplaces, muraled walls and a 48,000-gallon wine cellar. For much of the 20th century, the home served as a sanitarium, and it now operates as a popular historical attraction. As its nomination to the National Register of Historic Places put it, "It exemplifies the High Victorian taste for leaving no surface areas untouched."

VAUGHAN'S DIAMOND

This four-story landmark punctuated the prominent intersection of Main, Delaware and Ninth streets (opposite). Attributed to the architect Asa Beebe Cross, Vaughan's Diamond dates to 1869 or so and was a deft design solution to its narrow site, though, as George Ehrlich once wrote, "The aggregation of assorted decorative details might be labeled simply as Victorian excess." Perhaps foreshadowing the scrap-and-start-over ethos of later generations, the building was torn down in 1915; it gave way to a hotel project, which, in turn, was razed in 1954. The streets eventually were realigned, and the Muse of Missouri statue landed on the building's former spot in 1963.

WILLIAM VOLKER

Though he had hoped to remain anonymous as he gave away millions of dollars, German immigrant William Volker (1859-1947) is remembered all over town. A neighborhood, a college campus, a boulevard, a fountain, a River Market brick wall.

The merchant, philanthropist and towering civic leader brought his picture-frame business to Kansas City from Chicago in 1882 and grew it into a nationally known supplier of window shades. After bringing his family here, in 1889 Volker bought this 12-room house (architect unknown) at 3717 Bell St., and it remains a fine piece of history on a sprawling, landscaped lot.

Given his family's love for horticulture, his sister eventually named the estate Roselawn. With its brick-clad first floor and shingled second, the house is a classic representation of the "Kansas City shirtwaist" style.

VAN BRUNT

There've been at least four architects in Kansas City named Van Brunt, all of whom made significant contributions to the local landscape. Henry (1832-1903) was a Boston transplant and principal in the prominent firm of Van Brunt & Howe. Brothers Adriance (1836-1913) and John (1855-1924) were originally from New Jersey; they were Henry's contemporaries but apparently not related. Van Brunt Boulevard is named for Adriance, who was among the earliest proponents of Kansas City's parks and boulevard system (pictured is his Mission-inspired Swope Interpretative Center, 1905). John designed two notable park structures, the Paseo Pergola (1899) and the Gladstone Peristyle (1896), among other projects. Henry's son Courtland, who died in 1961, was best known for homes he designed in J.C. Nichols neighborhoods near Ward Parkway.

Henry Van Brunt, who tended toward classicism, was also a writer. He set down this bit of erudite reflection in 1893: "The power that elevates the science of building into the domain of architecture and makes it a fine art is the same power that converts prose into poetry. This is a creative power, which refines expression with beauty of form, and illuminates reason with imagination."

VML

When this advertising and marketing firm moved its headquarters (in 1996) into the city-owned terminal building at the Wheeler Downtown Airport, a stretch of "adaptive reuse" was in order. The task got bigger a few years later when it expanded into the first-level rotunda, incorporating the wide spiral staircase and what had been a longstanding civic event space. Now the agency operates in a sprawling, airy and playful series of cubicles and colorful work spaces. A long runway view of arriving aircraft and dignitaries certainly provides added value, if not creative inspiration.

VITAGRAPH FILM EXCHANGE BUILDING

Originally a warehouse that stored Warner Bros. films, this art deco-era structure at 1703 Wyandotte St. got new life in 2010 after a city-supported $24 million redevelopment and restoration project by philanthropist Shirley Bush Helzberg. The building now houses the administrative offices of the Kansas City Symphony and other tenants.

V

W

WHITTAKER U.S. COURTHOUSE

At least one local judge was appalled by the plan to build a new federal courthouse at a cost of $112 million. But all that's forgotten now, and the crescent-shaped building, clad in glass and precast concrete, remains one of the most distinctive on the downtown skyline. Designed by ASAI and Ellerbe Becket and opened in 1998, it sports many fine design details, including a three-story rotunda featuring silver-cloud granite walls, granite columns and a terrazzo floor. The Latin words for peace and law flank the south entry. The courthouse is named for the first judge from this area to serve on the Supreme Court; Charles Evans Whittaker, who died in 1973, served on the high court from 1957 to '62.

WILDER & WIGHT, WIGHT & WIGHT

The architectural firm of Wilder & Wight (established here in 1904) helped instill the Neo-Classical look in Kansas City. Among its lasting structures are the First National Bank Building (1904-06), now transformed as the Central Branch Library, at 10th Street and Baltimore Avenue, and the Livestock Exchange building (1910) in the West Bottoms. In 1911, Thomas Wight's younger brother, William, bought out partner Edward Wilder, and for the next three decades or so, Wight & Wight ruled: the Nelson-Atkins Museum of Art, Southeast High School, Jackson County Courthouse, Kansas City Life Insurance Co. and more. Across the civic mall from the Whittaker federal courthouse stands City Hall (1934), the brothers' classic art deco tower (left).

WHARF MASTER BUILDING

In an ongoing effort to reconnect people with the Missouri River, the Port Authority of Kansas City has a series of projects in the works and on the boards. The ASB Bridge Underpass lengthened the Riverfront Heritage hiking and biking trail. In the future, imagine this brick shell of a World War II-era railroad office building as a preserved ruin beneath some kind of tent or protective structure. The idea, according to the authority, is to create an indoor-outdoor event space adjacent to the trail, the river and restored riverbank ecosystems.

WYANDOTTE HIGH SCHOOL

Downtown Kansas City is often noted for its Depression-era building boom, but this eye-popping Kansas-side building was a product of the 1930s, too. The Chicago firm of Hamilton, Fellows and Nedved brought a stately, superbly detailed design to the brick structure in 1935, siting it to face the intersection of Minnesota Avenue and Washington Boulevard at an angle. KCK architect Joseph Radotinsky is also associated with the project. Landscape architects Hare and Hare designed the grounds.

WESTERN AUTO

Long past its usefulness as an advertising beacon in the night, the 1950s-era lighted sign on this office tower turned Grand Boulevard condo development has evolved into something else. But what? A commercial stamp on public space posing as something like art? A flattened cairn in the air to remind us where we've been and how to find our way into the future? A bit of urban poetry writ large? A civic landmark we can't live without? Kudos to those who keep its lights burning.

WESTHEIGHT MANOR
This historic subdivision in Kansas City, Kan., and its diverse collection of homes seems like a pattern book of middle-class American aspirations. The neighborhood, transected by Washington Boulevard and Hoel Parkway (21st Street), spans roughly 50 square blocks and includes Arts and Crafts bungalows, Spanish influences, big stone mansions and Prairie Style classics. The district was laid out by esteemed landscape design firm Hare and Hare. Among highlights are a couple of homes designed by Louis Curtiss: the Harry G. Miller Sr. house, from 1920-21 (left), and the former Jesse Hoel residence (right, 1916), named for the subdivision's developer. Top: the English-style grouping of frame and stucco homes called Westheight Court (1924), planned and designed by architects Edward Buehler Delk and Courtland Van Brunt.

W

WOODNEATH

In 2008, The Mid-Continent Public Library System acquired this antebellum Clay County homestead (1855-56) with the idea of incorporating it into a planned destination library. The brick, Greek Revival farmhouse, off Northeast Flintlock Road west of Liberty, will be shored up and remade inside to provide a formal entry and meeting spaces for a 35,000-square-foot library expected to be built in the coming years.

WALDO WATER TOWER

Since 1920, this reinforced concrete shaft has been a place-maker for the Waldo neighborhood near 75th Street and Holmes Road. Now locals are trying to raise upwards of $900,000 to preserve it and keep it a part of their identity. It long ago lost its usefulness as a water storage facility, but supporters clearly are hoping the tower, if rehabbed and kept alive, can remain a formidable landmark.

ST. FRANCIS XAVIER CATHOLIC CHURCH

Chicago architect Barry Byrne, known as one of the last practitioners of the Chicago School, teamed up with Joseph B. Shaughnessy of Kansas City to create one of the most distinctive mid-century buildings in the city. The fish-shaped structure, dominated by light Bedford stone and blue glass, points its tail – and its hoisted cross – toward the intersection of 52nd Street and Troost Avenue. The church, built for the quaint-sounding figure of $750,000 (less than $7 million in today's dollars), was dedicated on July 4, 1950. Out in front, the sculptural monument to the namesake 16th-century missionary was made by Alfonso Iannelli of Chicago.

X

CROSSROADS ARTS DISTRICT

X marks the spot (in the wayfaring sign) of this long-neglected part of downtown, which helped spur the city's urban revival of the last two decades. Artists and gallery owners, led by Jim and Sherry Leedy, began settling into the light industrial area in the mid-1980s, attracted by large, inexpensive digs in old warehouses and commercial buildings. The swarm followed, and soon the blocks surrounding 20th Street and Baltimore Avenue became the talk of the town among creative types. A few years ago, the energy expanded into the blocks east of Main Street.

DECORATIVE X

Yes, it's a cheap shortcut, but this timely and desperate discovery (opposite) appears in a decorative band above the entrance of a distinctively narrow downtown building. Opened in 1915 as the Hotel Bray ($1 a room and up) and later known as the New Yorker Inn, the nine-story structure at 1114 Baltimore St. (below) is 25 feet wide. The architect was John Martling, who worked in Kansas City from 1886 to 1930. The building is the smallest of seven downtown hotels submitted 30 years ago for a place on the National Historic Register.

X-BRACING

It could be one of the oldest tricks in the engineering playbook. X-shaped bracing is a logical solution for stiffening a box frame against lateral loads. You can find notable local expressions of the X in the ASB Bridge (above) and the tangly latticework of a midtown broadcast tower. In the latter half of the 20th century, the technology expanded to structural systems of skyscrapers, notably Chicago's John Hancock Center, the work of esteemed engineer Fazlur Khan of Skidmore, Owings and Merrill. Steve Huey, a principal of Wallace Engineering in Kansas City, called the Hancock tower "a 100-story monument to the righteousness and glory of the X brace." And, he quipped: "'Stability' being the most beloved concept of the structural engineer and 'dynamics' being the most beloved concept of the architect—the X brace is therefore the root of much tension between the building professions." No telling how much such tension arose, but a few years ago, Sir Norman Foster pumped up the X factor in the diamond-patterned exterior of the Hearst Tower in New York.

Y

YOUTHFUL EXUBERANCE

It's a long way from the confined penthouse elegance of, say, some old downtown men's club. But The Jones (left), with its poolside bars and skyline views, makes for a vibrant urban experience—at least for the folks the Power & Light District was built to attract.

Elsewhere in the city's fun spots, retractable, garage door windows (like these (above) at Willie's on Grand Boulevard) have become, if not a cliché, then a welcome, open-air enhancer for street-level experience. This is the worthy goal of urban placemakers: to bring people together in the great dance of democracy and enliven what planners, architects and dreamers like to call the public realm.

YANDA HOUSE

Architect Albert J. Yanda, a onetime student of Bruce Goff at the University of Oklahoma, built this midtown modern landmark for himself and his wife in 1966. The steel, aluminum and glass structure, an assemblage of simple geometrics, nestles into a cliff, its rear end a light-filled space overlooking Roanoke Park. The house is partly held up by stilts. (Hey, aren't those trusses shaped like a Y?) The plastic dome skylight reflects Yanda's adherence to a space-age ethos. He thought homes should be self-sustaining like space capsules. How far ahead of his time was he? In 1975, The Star featured Yanda and the prototype of a little electric car he designed and built. Americans waste far too much energy, he said, and largely because of our two-ton vehicles. The Yandas lived in the house, at 1102 Valentine Rd., for more than 20 years before retiring to California. He died in 2003. His widow, Emma Yanda, has nothing but fond memories of their home. "I just loved the openness," she said recently from Sun City, Ariz. "I think there was an ash tree below the balcony that turned yellow in the fall and our whole house turned this yellow blend." In the winter the couple sat under the dome to watch the snow fall.

YUM

New York architect David Rockwell is well known for creating one-of-a-kind restaurant atmospherics. In 1998 he set the bar for eatery design at a new level in these parts, creating a spacious and distinctive wine-bottle theme for Lidia's Kansas City in the renovated brick shell of an old railroad building renamed the Freight House. The soaring space of the main dining room includes timber trusses, lots of exposed brick, huge chandeliers made from glass shaped like rustic grappa bottles, and the glowing west wall evoking wine barrels and racks. Similarly ambitious interior makeovers were performed for two other Freight House restaurants—City Tavern (now Grunauer) and Fiorella's Jack Stack Barbecue.

ZAHNER

The metal fabrication firm of A. Zahner & Co. has been in business in Kansas City since about 1897. In the last decade, the firm's profile has gone global. Thanks go to star architects such as Frank Gehry, Thom Mayne and Rem Koolhaas, who have drawn on Zahner's expertise with metal in super-complicated systems to create some of the most daring buildings on the planet. To wit, and pictured here: the folding, colorful titanium skin of Gehry's Experience Music Project in Seattle (above, 2000); the perforated copper cladding at the De Young Museum in San Francisco (opposite page, 2005), designed by Herzog & de Meuron. In Kansas City, Zahner's high-profile work includes the R.M. Fischer "Sky Stations" atop the Bartle Hall pylons (1994), the new, gigantic crown scoreboard at Kauffman Stadium (2010) and the bead-blasted stainless steel roof for the Kauffman Center for the Performing Arts (2011).

In 2010 Zahner expanded its headquarters on the eastern edge of downtown. The building exterior carries this distinctive, wavy array of fins (above), which makes a sculptural and whimsical statement on the street front at Ninth Street and the Paseo.

ZONING
The idea that citizens and neighborhoods need protection from rampant, uncontrolled development is embodied in local zoning regulations. Kansas City's first zoning ordinance hit the books in 1923, when city boundaries contained barely 60 square miles. Now Kansas City, Mo., sprawls over five times that area, and, after a six-year revision effort, a new zoning and development ordinance is in place, passed in June 2010. (Find all 327 pages at the city's Web site: kcmo.org.) New features streamline some processes; sharpen standards relating to signage, landscaping, parking, pedestrian-enhancement and environmental issues; and help non-historic neighborhoods address development and preservation matters.

ZZZZZZZZZZZ
The stalled, slumbering West Edge office-hotel project—its fate currently in the hands of new owners—stands exposed and unfinished as a mocking testament to the consequences of hyper-inflated development dreams. It's Kansas City's leading example of the commercial real estate debacle that spread over the land. It also speaks to the all-too-common fragile complexity that underlies any relationship of owner, architect, builder and banker. Will the West Edge, designed by architect Moshe Safdie (and locals Gould Evans) ever be finished? Will it be demolished? It's odd that such a prominent failure has not been addressed by civic leaders. Here's hoping that some kind of progress will wake us from our West Edge nap by the time this book is published.

Acknowledgments

I've been writing about architecture off and on for a decade or so, not as an expert but, like many a journalist, as a curious student. I am indebted to the many architects and architectural historians I've gotten to know, hear and write about. Every encounter is a welcome learning experience. Although I've studied architecture casually for many years, my attention secured some keen focus in the 1980s and early '90s when I worked with Donald Hoffmann, The Star's former art and architecture critic. His careful eye and fearless commentary were inspiring. I also owe thanks to Mary Lou Nolan, The Star's assistant managing editor for features, who encouraged this series and made room for it in The Kansas City Star Magazine. Thanks also to designers Barbara Hill-Meyer and Neil Nakahodo, who helped make the series stand out in the magazine. In the transformation to this book, I am grateful to Doug Weaver, publisher of Kansas City Star Books, for his encouragement; to Diane McLendon, for her fine editing and commitment; and to Amy Robertson, whose design concept and engagement with the photos and text enlivened the project more than I could have imagined. Many readers offered ideas, feedback, guidance and corrections, all of which were appreciated. Any remaining errors are of my own doing. Lastly, many thanks to Carol Zastoupil, who also contributed vital ideas and went along on many weekend site visits and photo excursions. — SP

Sources/Picture Credits

Clipping files, digital archives and microfilm in The Kansas City Star's library were essential first stops in researching "Architecture A-Z." Other standard and very useful references included George Ehrlich's foundational work, "Kansas City, Missouri: An Architectural History, 1826-1990," published in 1992 (and referred to below as Ehrlich); "American Institute of Architects Guide to Kansas City Architecture & Public Art," published in 2000 (AIAKC); the physical and digital resources of the Kansas City Public Library's Missouri Valley Room Special Collections (KCPL); and the Kansas City Landmarks Commission's "A Place in Time," first published in 1977 and on the verge of an updated edition (KCLC). The National Parks Service online archives of National Register of Historic Places nomination applications proved to be a convenient outlet for mining the work of our area's meticulous architectural historians. Their documentation of historic properties and architects were indispensible. All of these sources and more are mentioned where appropriate on the following pages. In addition, photo credits are itemized for pictures taken or supplied by others.

A

Sprint Center arena photo by Keith Myers/The Star; Star; AIAKC; Port Authority of Kansas City; Kansas City Power & Light art deco panel photo by David Pulliam/The Star; airport photo from Star file.

B

Ehrlich; AIAKC; Missouri Department of Transportation; Star; Scott Lane and Robert McLaughlin, KCModern; "A Visual Dictionary of Architecture," by Francis D.K. Ching; National Park Service/National Register of Historic Places; Marcel Breuer Papers/Archives of American Art (online collection); historical Board of Trade and Hannibal Bridge, photos from Star file.

C

Denise DiPiazzo, former associate vice president of Gould Evans, contributed thoughts about concrete. AIAKC; Ehrlich; "Illustrated Dictionary of Architecture," by Ernest Burden; Star; KCPL; KCLC; Assassi/BNIM© (Omega photo); "Corinthian Hall: An American Palace on Gladstone," by Lenore K. Bradley (see the new, expanded edition, published in 2010 by Kansas City Star Books); Ehrlich; Michael Ray (see his blog on classical architecture: michaeljohnray.typepad.com/analytique).

D

Safdie (Kauffman Center drawing); Ehrlich; Star; AIAKC; Wyandotte County/Kansas City, Kan., Parks and Recreation; Kansas Historical Society ("Kansas Preservation"); Scott Lane, KCModern; KCPL.

E

AIAKC; Ehrlich; Star; KCPL; Steven Holl Architects (elevation).

F

Ehrlich; AIAKC; "There Is No Limit: Architecture and Sculpture in Kansas City," by Giles Carroll Mitchell (1934); Independence Tourism; Star; Unity Village/Jim Gillem (rendering); Truman Library, online oral history with Edgar C. Faris Jr.; Roland Sabates.

G

Ehrlich; Star; Mark Parsons; Greene & Greene Virtual Archives; Scott Lane, KC Modern; KCLC; AIAKC; architectural historians Cydney E. Millstein and Mary Ann Warfield.

H

Engineering News-Record; KCLC; Star; AIAKC; architectural historians Patricia Brown Glenn and Cydney E. Millstein; Ehrlich; Westport Historical Society; Sylvia Mooney.

I

Star; KCModern; Denise DiPiazzo; Ehrlich; "A Visual Dictionary of Architecture," by Francis D.K. Ching; "Corinthian Hall," by Lenore K. Bradley.

J

Star; Scott Lane, KCModern; Cydney E. Millstein; KCLC; Roy Inman/Powell Gardens (exterior chapel photo); Kansas State Historical Society; Wyandotte County; KCPL.

K

Ehrlich; Star; AIAKC; Susan Jezak Ford; Sherry Piland, Historic Kansas City Foundation newsletter; Charles E. Whitney, Architectural Forum; Mark Shapiro, Review magazine.

L

Ehrlich; Star; architectural historians Elisabeth Rosin, Janice Lee and others; “A City Within a Park: One Hundred Years of Parks and Boulevards in Kansas City, Missouri,” by Jane Mobley and Nancy Whitnell Harris; Susan Jezak Ford; KCLC.

M

Star; AIAKC; KCLC; Sue E. Yoakum; Grand Avenue Temple; Elizabeth Rosin; Ehrlich.

N

BNIM© (New Orleans rendering); Historic Kansas City Foundation; Star; Sally Schwenk; AIAKC; KCLC.

O

Star; Ehrlich; Populous.

P

Ehrlich; AIAKC; Star; Greenability magazine; Passive House Institute; Studio 804; McHenry Shaffer Mitchell Architects.

Q

Star, including Jones and Quindar file photos; AIAKC; “A Visual Dictionary of Architecture,” by Francis D.K. Ching; “The Grammar of Architecture,” edited by Emily Cole; Washington University Digital Library; eichlernetwork.com.

R

KCLC; Star; Ehrlich; Carol Cook, Topeka; George Birt; Scott Lane, KCModern; Kansas City Parks Department; Friends of the Rice-Tremonti Home (photos).

S

Star; Black & Veatch (dam photo); KCLC; AIAKC; Kansas City Parks Dept.

T

Star; Ehrlich; Cydney E. Millstein (TWA); www.buckminster.info and www.kennethsnelson.net; Matt Gearhart, Gastinger Walker Harden; AIAKC.

U

Star; Mike Sinclair/El Dorado (Unitarian Fellowship photos); KCLC; University of Kansas Hospital.

V

Star, including Vaughn’s Diamond file photo; AIAKC; Ehrlich; National Parks Service/National Register of Historic Places; KCLC; KCPL.

W

Star; KCPL; Mid-Continent Public Library (Woodneath photos); Ehrlich; AIAKC; Cydney Millstein (“Westheight Manor Historic Survey”); Kansas City, Kan., Public Schools.

X

Star; “A Visual Dictionary of Architecture,” by Francis D.K. Ching; Steve Huey, Wallace Engineering. KCLC.

Y

Star, including Lidia’s file photo; Jennifer Hack (The Jones photo); KCLC.

Z

Star; Kansas City Planning and Development Dept.; Ehrlich.

About the Author

Steve Paul has been a writer and editor at The Kansas City Star since 1975. He is a native of Boston and graduate of the University of Missouri-Kansas City. In 2009 the American Institute of Architects/Kansas City named him Architectural Advocate of the Year. He is also the co-editor of "War & Ink," a collection of essays about Ernest Hemingway's early years (forthcoming from Kent State University Press) and editor of "Kansas City Noir," a collection of short fiction to be published by Akashic Books in 2012.

Index

Italic page numbers indicate photographs

ESTE
AUT